YOU CAN MAKE IT!
YOU CAN DO IT!

101 E-Z Holiday Craf-tivities for Children

Written and Compiled by
Ann Peaslee
&
Jullien Kille

Illustrations by
Dave Ball

Heian

You Can Make It!   You Can Do It!
101 E-Z Holiday Craf-tivities for Children

Text by Ann Peaslee and Jullien Kille
Illustration by Dave Ball

© 1990, Ann Peaslee and Jullien Kille
© 1990, Illustration, Dave Ball

ISBN: 0-89346-337-X

HEIAN INTERNATIONAL
P.O. BOX 1013
UNION CITY, CA 94587   USA

91 92 93 94   10 9 8 7 6 5 4 3 2 1

Manufactured in the United States of America

Dedicated to

Sue Story

*who unlocks the genius in
every mind she touches*

SPECIAL THANKS TO:

Pat Fox for her special touches and typing, Liz Herrera for her great ideas, Jan Ball who kept Dave going with back scratches, Butch Kille for our killer title, and Don Peaslee, because he was the wind beneath our wings.

YOU CAN MAKE IT!   YOU CAN DO IT!
101 E-Z Holiday Craf-tivities for Children

ABOUT THIS BOOK:

This collection of holiday craftivities is an informal compilation of ideas, experiences and insights from many years of working with children. It is presented in response to a constant cry for fresh, new, quick and easy holiday art activities for young children. A wealth of information and ideas are now at your fingertips for easy use and immeasurable amounts of enjoyment.

It has taken many years to promote the acceptance of art activities as having importance in enhancing a child's total development. While researchers have repeatedly provided clear evidence that young children learn best by doing, providing success through creative art experiences will promote a healthier emotional climate for young children. The ideas for these craftivities have been selected because they have value in helping children learn, rather than just keeping them busy.

These holiday craftivities are suggested for anyone sharing time with children (e.g. parents, grandparents, teachers, counselors, scout leaders, day care workers, church group leaders, etc.). It is recognized that each situation is unique, and in writing this book many versatile ideas have been presented. Most of the activities require minimal adult planning and it is up to you to choose those activities that will work for you—dip in and adapt the ideas to fit your own situation. The craftivity ideas are easily adjusted for children of all ages, to be done alone or in groups.

The most important aspect of all of these holiday craftivities is not the finished product but rather the actual doing. It is hoped these suggestions and ideas will help to expand your repertoire of activities for young children as well as encourage all of us to take time from the daily rush to stop and share life with young children.

Enjoy ...

Sue Story
Program Manager
Southern Alameda County Head Start Program
Fremont, California

ACKNOWLEDGMENTS

Amanda Bauer

Erin Bennett

Steve Beauson

Tracy Blincoe

Mike Brysek

Eileen Burns

Scott Carlsen

Zack Chedwick

Saunders Ching

Alicia Cox

Thomas Elliott

Chris Ferreira

Andrew Heywood

Brian Hockenberger

Chris King

David Huang

Darrell Lam

Paige Landman

Jason Liou

Karen Luk

Nathan Mara

Katie Marshall

Meredith Mathiesen

Georgine Moffit

Ruby Multani

Megan Munay

Bradley Oats

Shanna Marie O'Neill

Angela Parenti

Neha Parekh

Richard Peaslee

Felicia Pedraza

Ann Power

Jill Ravenelle

Carrie Rossetti

Sean Segel

Louisa Sena

Lena Sharma

Robbie Shoplock

Ryan Smith

Kara Staal

Zack Taylor

Exerson Thompson

Paul Trowbridge

Mario Ventimiglio

Barbara Walter

Jeremy Welch

Jessica Wu

Jennifer Yen

Ben Zweig

TABLE OF CONTENTS

HOLIDAYS REPRESENTED:

New Year's Day
Abraham Lincoln's Birthday
Valentine's Day
George Washington's Birthday
St. Patrick's Day
Easter
May Day
Mother's Day
Father's Day
Independence Day
Birthdays
Back to School
American Indian Day
Halloween
Thanksgiving
Hanukkah
Christmas
Sick Days

SUGGESTED ART MATERIALS

The California Department of Health Services has prepared a "Program Advisory with Guidelines for Safe Use of Art and Craft Materials" which addresses special concerns for choosing materials for programs for young children. The guide advises avoiding the following substances and suggests acceptable alternatives:

AVOID:	SUBSTITUTE:
Clay in dry form (silica or asbestos inhalation hazard)	Clay in wet form
Prints, glazes, or finishes that contain lead or other metal pigments	Water-based products
Organic solvents and materials with fumes	Water-based paints, glues, etc.
Commercial dyes	Vegetable dyes
Permanent markers	Water-based markers
Instant papier-mache or use of color print newspaper or magazines with water (lead and other metals in color print inks)	Papier-mache made from black and white newspaper
Aerosol sprays	Water-based materials
Powdered tempera paints (toxic dust)	Liquid paints

SPRING

Cotton Ball Sachet

Easter Bunny Salad

Hat Parade

Hatched Chick

Jelly Bean Hunt

Jelly Bean Race

May Basket

Pin the Tail on the Bunny

Scrambled Eggs

Shamrock Artist

Special Magnet

Terrarium

Tie-Dyed Wrapping Paper

□o COTTON BALL SACHET

Materials You Need:

- 6-inch square of fine lace material
- 18-inch piece of narrow ribbon
- 6 cotton balls
- Perfume in spray bottle*

How You Make It:

1. Lay six cotton balls together in the center of the lace material.
2. Spray the cotton balls lightly with perfume.
3. Bring ends of lace together over cotton balls and tie firmly with ribbon.
4. Tie ribbon into a bow.
5. If perfume begins to fade away, just spray again lightly through the lace.

*Be careful not to spray into your eyes.

Bo EASTER BUNNY SALAD

Materials You Need:

- 1 pear half
- Whipped cream
- 3 raisins
- 1 marshmallow
- 2 thin apple wedges
- Salad plate covered with a lettuce leaf
- Shredded coconut
- Knife

How You Make It:

1. Lay the pear half, cut side down, on a salad plate covered with a lettuce leaf.
2. Lightly cover the pear half with whipped cream.
3. Attach a marshmallow at the large end of the pear to form a tail.
4. Attach three raisins for eyes and nose to the narrow end of the pear.
5. Cut two slits in the top of the pear just behind the eyes and attach the two thin apple slices for ears.
6. Lightly sprinkle the pear bunny with shredded coconut for a furry effect.
7. Eat and enjoy.

4

ℬo HAT PARADE

Materials You Need:

- Paper plate
- 1-inch wide ribbon, 36 inches long
- Scissors
- Tape
- Glue
- Decorator items (see step 3 below)

How You Make It:

1. Cut a one-inch slit on each side of the bottom of a paper plate.

2. Push one end of the ribbon through one slit and the other end of the ribbon through the other slit. Pull ribbon snugly through slits. This ribbon will hold the hat on your head and tie under your chin.

3. Now decorate the top of your hat with silk flowers, ribbons, bows, small toys, or whatever else you can think of.

4. After you and your friends have created your hats, you can have a fashion parade.

⊞o HATCHED CHICK

Materials You Need:

- 1 egg shell, broken in half
- 2 large cotton balls, white or colored
- Glue
- 2 small wiggly eyes from craft store
- Small piece of yellow or orange construction paper
- Scissors

How You Make It:

1. Wash the inside of the broken egg shell carefully.
2. Put a drop of glue inside the bottom of one egg shell half.
3. Insert a cotton ball.
4. Put a drop of glue on top of the cotton ball in the egg shell.
5. Gently press a second cotton ball on top of the first cotton ball. Let dry.
6. Put glue on the back sides of the wiggly eyes and attach to the top cotton ball to form eyes. Let dry.
7. Cut a small triangle shape from the construction paper. Fold in half lengthwise.
8. Attach the triangle with glue to form a beak. Let dry.
9. Put a drop of glue on the inside of the remaining broken egg shell.
10. Set the egg shell on top of the chick's head. Let dry.

HOW DO I GET OUT OF THIS CHICKEN OUTFIT?

5 JELLY BEAN HUNT

Materials You Need:

- Jelly beans (2 colors only)
- Easter basket
- 8 or more children

How You Do It:

1. Hide jelly beans around the room. Use only two colors of jelly beans.

2. Divide children into two teams. One team will hunt for one color jelly bean, and the other team will hunt for the other color.

3. One child from each team becomes a bunny.

4. At a given time, all children hunt for their jelly beans. When they find one, they call their bunny to pick it up. Only the bunny can pick up a jelly bean and the bunny can only pick up his team's color jelly bean.

5. The bunny returns his jelly bean to the Easter basket and his team continues to find the rest of their jelly beans. Remember, only the bunny can pick up the jelly beans.

6. The game continues for a set amount of time, and the team with the most jelly beans in the basket wins.

SHHHHHH!
BE VERWY, VERWY
QWIET... WEAH
HUNTING JELWY
BEANS.

SNIFF
SNIFF

60 JELLY BEAN RACE

Materials You Need:

- 2 bowls of jelly beans
- 2 empty bowls
- 2 tablespoons
- 8 or more children

How You Do It:

1. Divide children into two teams. Have each team line up one behind the other.
2. Place the bowls of jelly beans on a table at the front of the teams.
3. Place the two empty bowls across the room (or across the yard, if playing outside).
4. The first child in each line takes a tablespoon and scoops as many jelly beans onto his/her spoon as it will hold.
5. The children then carry the spoon of jelly beans across the room (or yard) and drop the jelly beans into the empty bowl. If a jelly bean falls off the spoon, the child must go back to the beginning and start over.
6. After the child drops the jelly beans in the bowl across the room (or yard) he/she runs back to his/her team and passes the spoon to his/her teammate.
7. The game continues until everyone has had a turn.
8. The team with the most transported jelly beans wins.

7o MAY BASKET

Materials You Need:

- Ice cream cone
- Assorted candies
- Plastic wrap
- 4 feet of narrow ribbon, cut into two 2-foot lengths
- Scissors

How You Make It:

1. Fill an empty ice cream cone with assorted candies.
2. Cut a large circle from plastic wrap and lay over top of the candy-filled cone.
3. Tie two narrow ribbons around the top rim and knot at opposite sides.
4. Bring the four ends up and tie together in a bow to form a handle.

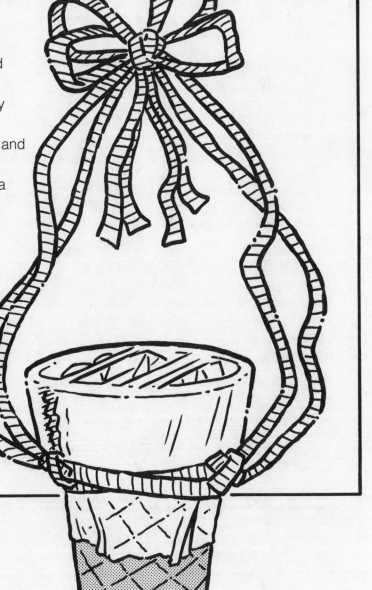

8. PiN THE TAiL ON THE BUNNY

Materials You Need:

- 1 sheet of 8½" x 11" typing paper
- Pencil
- Scissors
- Large cotton ball for each child
- 1 piece of tape per cotton ball
- Scarf for blindfold

How You Do It:

1. Draw a large bunny on piece of typing paper.

2. Cut out the bunny, and tape it to the wall.

3. Cut a piece of tape about one inch long for each cotton ball.

4. Fold tape over to form a loop and attach to cotton ball.

5. Each child takes a turn and tries to attach his/her cotton ball tail to the bunny while being blindfolded.

6. The child with the best-looking bunny wins.

UH... CLOETH KID, BUT NO THIGAR.

🐰 SCRAMBLED EGGS

Materials You Need:

- Pencil
- "Scrambled Eggs" game

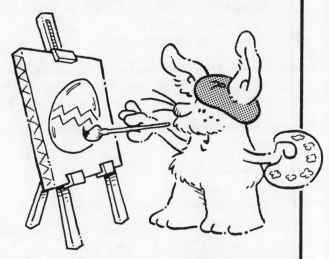

How You Do It:

Unscramble the Easter eggs to find Easter-related words. Answers on page 125.

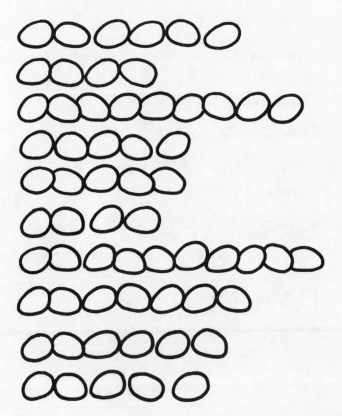

TSKBEA

GSGE

LTECOHCOA

SRAGS

IHCKC

IYLL

SBLJNAEEYL

THGEUGN

TBNEON

NYNUB

▣⊙○ SHAMROCK ARTiST

Materials You Need:

- Large sheets of green construction paper
- 2 or more children

How You Do It:

1. Give each child a piece of green construction paper.
2. Have the children hold the paper behind their backs and try to tear out a shamrock.
3. Give a prize to the child whose creation looks most like a shamrock.

UH... WELL... I GUESS I'VE GOT THE "ROCK" PART... NOW I JUST GOTTA FIGURE OUT THE "SHAM" PART.

☐☐₀ SPECIAL MAGNET

Materials You Need:

- 2-inch square of construction paper
- 3-inch square of construction paper
- Small school photo of child
- Glue
- Scissors
- Small sticky-back magnet (available at craft stores)
- Felt-tip pen, pencil, or crayons

How You Make It:

1. Fold the two-inch square of construction paper in half and cut out half a heart shape on the folded side. Remove the heart.

2. Open the paper to form a heart-shaped window.

3. Glue the school photo edges to the window so the picture shows through the heart. Let dry.

4. Glue the photo window to the three-inch square of construction paper being sure to get it centered. Let dry.

5. On the top of the three-inch square, print *"Mom is Special."*

6. On the bottom of the three-inch square, print *"She has Me!"*

7. Attach the sticky-back magnet to the back of the finished photo.

More Ideas for You:

Special magnet may be made for Dad, Gramma, or any family member by changing the *"Mom"* title.

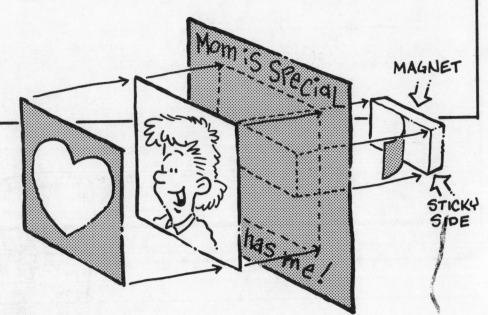

13. TERRARIUM

Materials You Need:

- Glass jar
- Modeling clay
- Dried or silk flowers with stems
- Moss
- Ribbon or lace
- Glue

How You Make It:

1. Place a piece of modeling clay in the lid of a glass jar.

2. Arrange dried or silk flowers with stems in the clay.

3. Place the jar over the flower arrangement and tighten the lid.

4. Spread glue around the edge of the lid and trim with ribbon or lace.

14

□3◦ TiE-DYED WRAPPiNG PAPER

Materials You Need:

- 2 sheets tissue paper
- 4 cereal bowls filled with water
- Food coloring (4 colors)
- Newspaper

How You Make It:

1. Place two sheets of tissue paper together.

2. Fold paper many times until you have a 2" by 4" rectangle.

3. Add a few drops of food coloring to each bowl of water until you have achieved desired color.

4. Dip one corner of paper into one dish of colored water.

5. Repeat dipping each corner in a different color.

6. When all four corners of paper have been dipped, carefully open and allow to dry on newspaper.

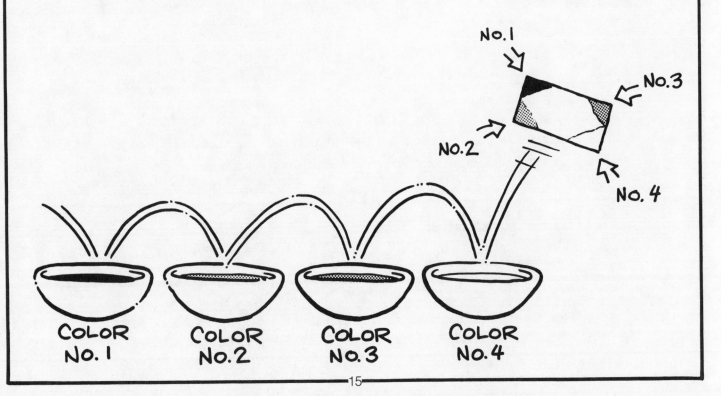

SUMMER

Autograph Book
Breakfast Bake
Cookie Pops
Dad's Castle
Designer Bank
Doggie Grrrraham Crackers
Fingerprint/Footprint Art
Get Well Bag
Get Well Chain
Half Birthday
Paper House
Paper Plate Puppet
Peanut Puppets
Personalized Greeting Card
Picnic Caterpillar Yummies
Popcorn Fireworks
Puppy Party
Sand Timer
Snail Race
Stamp Art
Star Spangled Dessert

14. AUTOGRAPH BOOK

Materials You Need:

- 6 or more sheets of construction paper
- Single-hole paper punch
- Yarn
- Scissors
- Crayons or felt-tip pens

How You Make It:

1. Fold construction paper in fourths.
2. Cut paper along fold lines.
3. Punch two holes along one side of each piece of paper, being careful to punch all holes in the same place.
4. Put all punched papers together and tie together with yarn.
5. Color the cover page.
6. Pass the book around for all your friends to sign.

15. BREAKFAST BAKE

Materials You Need:

- Mixing bowl
- Fork
- 6 eggs
- 1 cup milk
- 1 teaspoon dry mustard
- Salt and pepper
- 1 cup grated cheddar cheese
- 1/2 pound fried and crumbled bacon or sausage
- 3 green onions, chopped
- French bread
- Butter
- 9" x 13" baking pan

How You Make It:

1. Spread butter in the baking pan so the "Breakfast Bake" won't stick.

2. Tear french bread into small pieces and cover bottom of baking pan.

3. Mix the eggs, milk, dry mustard, salt, and pepper with a fork in mixing bowl.

4. Pour egg mixture over the bread pieces.

5. Sprinkle bacon or sausage over the bread-egg mixture.

6. Sprinkle cheese over the bacon or sausage.

7. Bake at 350 degrees for about 40 minutes or till not runny anymore.

8. Slice into large squares. This makes a great breakfast in bed for Mom or Dad. Serve with juice and fresh fruit.

* BIRTHDAY, ANNIVERSARY VALENTINE'S DAY, BARMITZVAH...ETC.

** MOM, DAD, SIGNIFICANT OTHER...

20

16. COOKIE POPS

Materials You Need:

- 1 roll of refrigerated cookie dough
- Wooden popsicle sticks
- Cookie sheet
- Cooling rack
- Knife
- Decorator frosting tubes

How You Make It:

1. Cut refrigerator cookie dough into slices.

2. Insert a wooden popsicle stick into each cookie slice.

3. Place cookie pops on a cookie sheet and bake at 350 degrees for 12 to 15 minutes.

4. Remove baked cookie pops from oven and let cool on cooling racks.

5. Decorate cookie pops with frosting tubes.

6. Eat and enjoy.

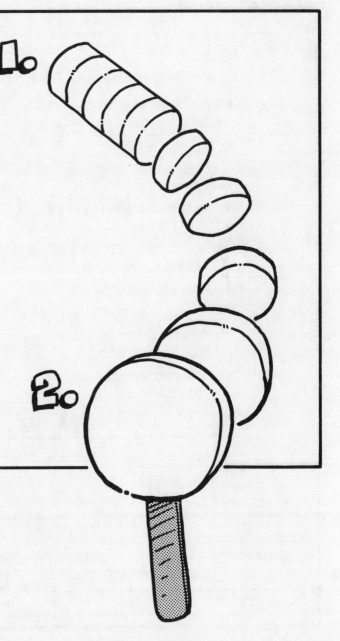

17. DAD'S CASTLE

Materials You Need:

- 12-inch round tray or plate
- 12 to 14-inch paper doily
- $\frac{1}{2}$ gallon ice cream, any flavor, in rectangular container
- $\frac{1}{2}$ gallon ice cream, any flavor, in round container
- 2 packages sugar wafers
- 5 or 6 cookies of assorted shapes
- Colored construction paper
- 4 sugar cones
- 1 tube of frosting
- 1 cherry
- Sharp knife
- 3 toothpicks
- Scissors
- Glue

How You Make It:

1. Cover tray or plate with paper doily.

2. Remove cartons from ice cream by cutting with a knife down the sides of container and pulling them away from the ice cream.

3. Lay rectangular-shaped ice cream on its side onto the center of the paper doily.

4. Stand the round-shaped ice cream on top of the rectangular-shaped ice cream.

5. Press sugar wafers onto all of the ice cream sides to create a stone-wall effect.

6. Stack four sugar cones on top of one another on the round-shaped ice cream to form a tower.

7. Top tower with a cherry.

8. Cut three small triangular flags out of colored construction paper.

9. Glue flags to toothpicks.

10. Insert one flag on top of cherry tower. Insert two flags on castle roof.

11. Spread frosting on back of cookies and attach to castle walls to form door and windows.

12. Put castle in freezer for about one hour before eating.

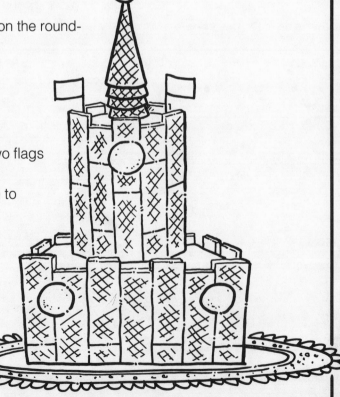

18. DESIGNER BANK

Materials You Need:

- 2-pound coffee can with plastic lid
- Construction paper
- Crayons or felt-tip pens
- Scissors
- Glue
- Knife

How You Make It:

1. Cut a piece of construction paper 6½ inches by 17 inches.

2. Draw a picture or designs on the paper.

3. Spread glue on the back side of the paper and attach to the can. Let dry.

4. Put the lid on the can and cut a slit in it big enough so coins will slide through.

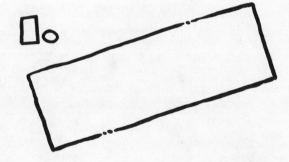

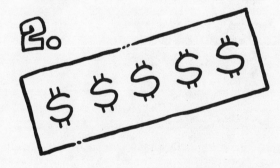

19. DOGGY GRRRRAHAM CRACKERS

Materials You Need:

- ³/₄ cup graham flour
- ¹/₂ cup bran or corn meal
- 1 cup whole wheat flour
- ¹/₂ teaspoon salt
- ¹/₂ cup water
- 6 tablespoons vegetable oil
- 1 tablespoon molasses
- Mixing bowl
- Spoon
- Cookie pan
- Rolling pin
- Knife

How You Make It:

1. Preheat oven to 350 degrees.

2. Mix all ingredients together in a bowl until dough sticks together.

3. Pat the dough into the cookie pan.

4. With rolling pin, roll out the dough to a thickness of ¹/₈ inch.

5. Bake at 350 degrees for 12 to 15 minutes. Remove from oven.

6. Immediately cut into doggy bite-size crackers. Let cool. Store in glass jar.

30. FINGER PRINT - FOOT PRINT ART

Materials You Need:

- Finger paints, assorted colors
- White construction paper
- Newspaper
- Paper towels
- Paint brush
- 1 bare foot
- Fingers

How You Do It:

1. Cover work area with newspaper.

2. Spread finger paint on the bottom of your bare foot with your fingers.

3. Gently press your footprint onto the white construction paper. Remove your foot and wipe off the excess paint with paper towels. Let footprint dry.

4. Study the footprint. What imaginary animal or shape do you see? A footprint can become a bird or a fish or even a ghost.

5. Finish the creation by adding an eye, nose, mouth, fin, wing, or whatever else it may need.

6. Smaller animal or flower creations can be made by using fingerprints. A fingerprint may become a bird, mouse, bunny, center of a flower, leaves on a tree, etc.

ACTUAL DEMONSTRATION PROJECT DONE BY THE ARTIST'S DAUGHTER, CAITIE BALL

bird

caitie

30. GET WELL BAG

Materials You Need:

- Paper lunch bag
- Apple
- Can of chicken noodle soup
- Small bottle of aspirin
- Packet of tissues
- Felt-tip pen

How You Make It:

1. Write a get-well message on the outside of a paper lunch bag. Decorate the bag with drawings of flowers, hearts, or smiling faces.

2. Fill the bag with an apple, a can of chicken noodle soup, aspirin, tissues, and anything else a sick friend might need or like, such as cough drops or a magazine.

22. GET WELL CHAIN

Materials You Need:

- Construction paper (assorted colors)
- Stapler with staples
- Pencils, crayons, or felt-tip pens
- Scissors

How You Make It:

1. Cut construction paper into 2" by 11" strips.
2. Have friends and family members write messages or draw pictures on the paper strips.
3. Staple the strips together to form a chain.
4. Present the chain to a sick friend.

23. HALF BIRTHDAY

Materials You Need:

- Paper birthday plates
- Paper birthday napkins
- Paper cups
- Scissors
- Birthday balloons
- Birthday cake
- Ice cream
- Knife
- Ice cream scoop
- Plastic forks or spoons
- Juice

How You Make It:

1. Cut paper plates and napkins in half. Cut birthday cake in half.

2. Set table with $\frac{1}{2}$ paper plates, $\frac{1}{2}$ napkins, cups, and forks or spoons.

3. Fill cups only half full with juice.

4. Set $\frac{1}{2}$ cake in center of table. Serve cake on $\frac{1}{2}$ plates with $\frac{1}{2}$ scoop of ice cream.

5. Decorate the room with half-blown up balloons.

6. Sing only half a verse of "Happy Birthday to You."

7. Give half presents; for example, one sock, one glove, one slipper, birthday cards cut in half, etc.

BIRTHDAYS ARE GREAT AND ALL... BUT AS I GET OLDER, I JUST DON'T FEEL LIKE I'M HALF THE KID I USED TO BE...

24. PAPER HOUSE

Materials You Need:

- Construction paper
- Scissors
- Crayons

How You Do It:

1. Fold the paper in half with the fold on the side.

2. Cut off the two corners at the top of the folded sheet. This will form the roof of the house.

3. Draw the doors and windows and color the outside.

4. Open the house and draw a picture of your family. A message can also be included on the inside and the paper house can be used as a greeting card.

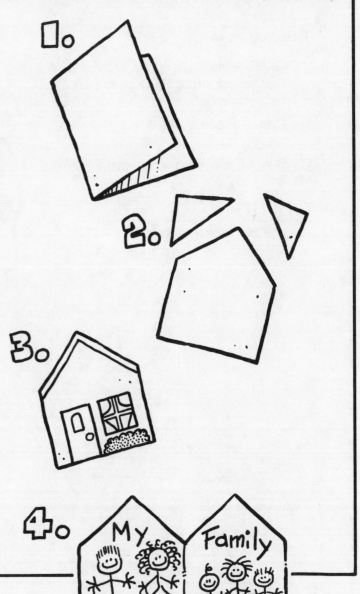

25. PAPER PLATE PUPPET

Materials You Need:

- Small paper plates
- Wooden ice cream sticks or tongue depressors
- Crayons or felt-tip pens
- Glue
- Buttons, yarn, ribbon, or lace (optional)

How You Make It:

1. Glue a small paper plate to the end of a wooden ice cream stick or tongue depressor. Let dry.

2. Create a face on the paper plate with crayons or felt-tip pens.

3. Buttons may be glued in place for eyes and yarn may be used for hair.

4. Be creative.

26. PEANUT PUPPETS

Materials You Need:

- Peanuts in the shell
- Felt-tip pens

How You Make It:

1. Break an end off a peanut shell. Remove the peanuts and eat.

2. Draw a face on the largest end of the shell and slip over your finger.

3. Draw faces on five shells, slip on your fingers, and have a peanut family.

HOW DO I GET OUT OF THIS "NUTTY" FAMILY?

More Ideas for You:

Have friends make "Peanut Puppets" and put on a puppet show.

27. PERSONALIZED GREETING CARD

Materials You Need:

- 1 sheet of white construction paper
- Crayons or felt-tip pens
- Scissors
- Photo of child
- Glue

How You Make It:

1. Fold construction paper in half to form a card.

2. Cut a square, circle, or heart out of the center of the front side of the card just large enough so photo will show through.

3. Glue the photo to the inside of the card, being careful to position it so it shows through the cover window. Let dry.

4. With crayons or felt-tip pens, decorate the cover. Perhaps the photo could become the center of a sun or flower.

5. Write a message on the inside of the card above and below the photo.

STEP 1.

STEP 2.

STEP 3.

STEP 4.

28. PICNIC CATERPILLAR YUMMIES

Materials You Need:

- 4-inch pieces of cleaned celery
- Peanut butter
- Sunflower seeds
- Spoon
- Party toothpicks (with frilly ends)
- Raisins

How You Make It:

1. Fill celery pieces with peanut butter.
2. Poke sunflower seeds into bottom sides of celery to form legs.
3. Attach two party toothpicks to one end of celery to form antennae.
4. Attach two raisins for eyes.
5. Eat and enjoy. Yum, yum.

29. POPCORN FIREWORKS

Materials You Need:

- Electric popcorn popper *(needs adult supervision)*
- Popcorn
- Clean sheet
- Large paper bag
- Melted butter
- Salt

How You Make It:

1. Spread a clean sheet on the floor.
2. Place the popcorn popper in the middle of the sheet.
3. Have an adult plug in the popcorn popper.
4. Fill the necessary compartment of the popcorn popper according to the manufacturer's directions.
5. Leave the lid off the popper.
6. Sit back away from the popcorn popper so you won't get burned and watch the popcorn fireworks.
7. When the popcorn has finished popping, put all the popcorn in a large paper bag.
8. Add melted butter and salt to taste.
9. Eat and enjoy.

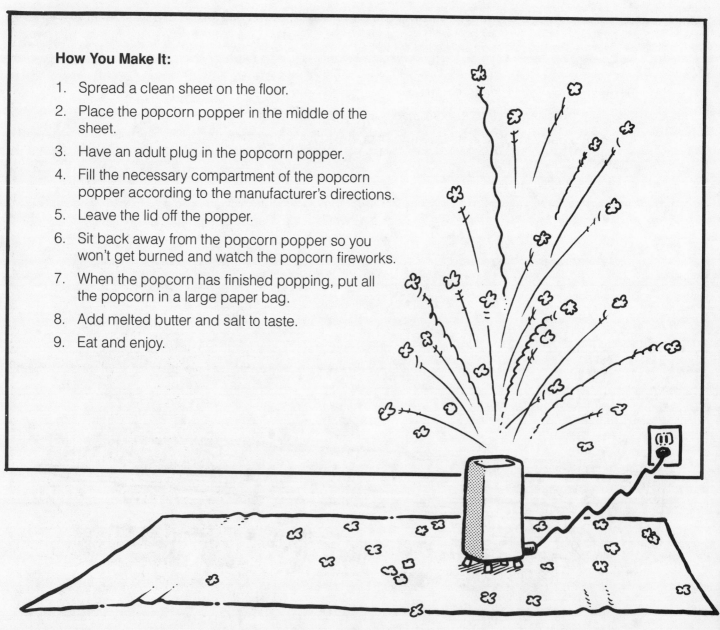

30. PUPPY PARTY

Materials You Need:

- Party hats and balloons
- Party plates, napkins, and forks
- Ice cream and scoop
- Dog food burgers
- Birthday candle
- Felt-tip pen
- Birthday cake made in dog-shaped pan (available at party supply stores)
- "Doggy Grrrraham Crackers" (recipe on p.24)
- Plastic sandwich bags

How You Do It:

1. This birthday party is the same as any birthday party, however, the guest of honor is your family pet.

2. Write your pet's name on the party hats and balloons.

3. Everyone wears a hat, including your pet.

4. Decorate the room and the table with the balloons.

5. Make a special birthday cake for your pet by putting a candle in a dog food burger.

6. If you invite your friends' pets, be sure to have a Gaines Burger cake for each one.

7. Make the "Doggy Grrrraham Crackers" on page   and put some in a plastic "doggie bag" for the pets to take home.

8. While the pets eat their special burger cakes, you may eat your cake and ice cream.

More Ideas for You:

Sing "How Much is That Doggie in the Window."

30. SAND TIMER

Materials You Need:

- 2 small jars with lids that are the same size
- Hammer
- Nail
- Sand or salt
- Glue

How You Make It:

1. With a hammer and nail, punch a hole in the center of both jar lids. Make sure both holes are the same size and in the same place.

2. Glue the lid tops together being careful to line up the holes. Let dry.

3. Fill one jar nearly full with sand or salt.

4. Screw both jars onto the caps. Sand timer may be used for timing games.

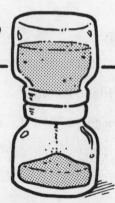

32. SNAIL RACE

Materials You Need:

- Children
- Bicycles

How You Do It:

1. Children on bicycles line up at a starting line.

2. When a signal is given, the racers go as slowly as they can to the finish line. No one is allowed to put his/her foot on the ground before reaching the finish line.

3. The rider who crosses the finish line last wins.

33. STAMP ART

Materials You Need:

- Dense sponge
- Styrofoam egg carton lid
- Pencil
- Paper
- Scissors
- Glue
- Wood blocks
- Ink pads with colored ink

How You Make It:

1. Draw and cut out a design on a piece of paper (flower, heart, star, animal, leaf, etc.).
2. Trace design onto sponge or styrofoam egg carton lid.
3. Cut out design.
4. Glue the design on a wooden block. Let dry.
5. Press design end into ink-filled pad. (When stamping washable items, use permanent ink.)
6. Stamp wrapping paper, gift bags, baskets, paper, cards, fabric, boxes, folders, etc.

34. STAR SPANGLED DESSERT

Materials You Need:

- Watermelon wedges with rind removed
- Vanilla ice cream
- Ice cream scoop
- Blueberries
- Dessert plate

How You Make It:

1. Place a single scoop of vanilla ice cream in the center of a dessert plate.

2. Arrange five watermelon wedges around the ice cream to form a star design.

3. Sprinkle blueberries over the ice cream.

KIDS! DON'T DO THIS AT HOME... OR YOU'LL HAVE "STAR SPANGLED DESSERT" ALL OVER THE FLOOR...

FALL

Autumn Art
Autumn Decorator Plate
Autumn Mobile
Bird Feeder
Indian Trail Mix
Jack O Lantern Cookies
Monster Match
Nature's Window
Pencil Ghosts
Pumpkin Cake
Pumpkin Match
Pumpkin Vase
Spider Cupcakes
Spooky Fill-In
Styro Spider
Sweet Potato Vine
T-H-A-N-K-S-G-I-V-I-N-G Game
Totem Pole
Turkey Trot
Walnut Mouse

35. AUTUMN ART

Materials You Need:

- Autumn leaves (fresh—dry leaves will crumble)
- Thin white paper
- Crayons

How You Do It:

1. Place a piece of thin white paper over a leaf. Hold the paper firmly over the leaf with one hand so it does not slide.
2. Color over the paper-covered leaf with the side of a crayon.
3. Lift the paper and remove the leaf.
4. Repeat with different shapes of leaves.

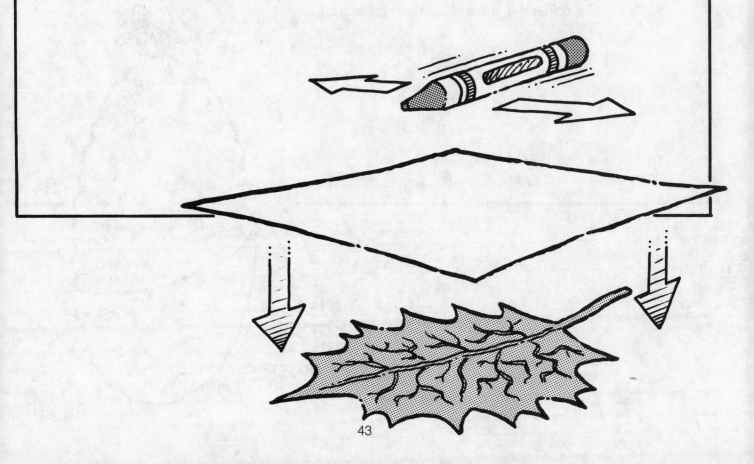

36. AUTUMN DECORATOR PLATE

Materials You Need:

- 2 paper plates
- Two 12-inch pieces of yarn for hanger
- Glue
- Single-hole paper punch
- Dried flowers and autumn leaves
- Scissors

How You Make It:

1. Cut one paper plate in half. Set aside.

2. Punch two holes about $1\frac{1}{2}$ inches apart from one another on one edge of whole plate.

3. Attach yarn through holes to form a hanger.

4. Glue the half paper plate onto the bottom half of the whole paper plate to form a pocket. Let dry.

5. Fill the holder with dried flowers and autumn leaves.

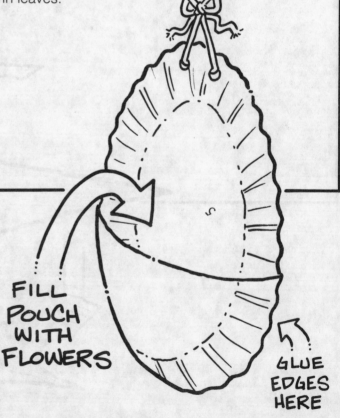

FILL POUCH WITH FLOWERS

GLUE EDGES HERE

37o AUTUMN MOBILE

Materials You Need:

- Coat hanger
- String
- Scissors
- Autumn leaves and pine cones

How You Make It:

1. Go for a walk and collect autumn leaves and pine cones.

2. Attach string to the end of colored leaves and pine cones.

3. Tie the stringed leaves and pine cones to the bottom of a coat hanger.

4. Hang the "Autumn Mobile" in your room.

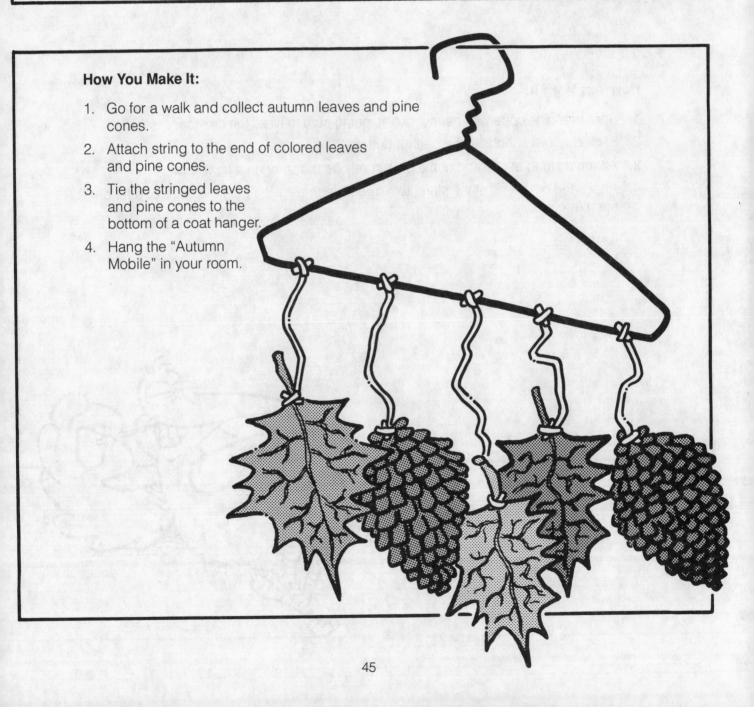

45

38. BiRD FEEDER

Materials You Need:

- Large pine cone
- Peanut butter
- Sunflower seeds
- Knife
- String

How You Make It:

1. Spread a pine cone with peanut butter, being sure to fill all the crevices.
2. Stick sunflower seeds in the peanut butter.
3. Attach a string at one end of the pine cone. Tie the string in a tight knot.
4. Attach the other end of the string to a tree branch allowing the pine cone bird feeder to hang freely.

46

39. INDIAN TRAIL MIX

Materials You Need:

- ½ cup measuring cup
- Any five of the following ingredients:

Sunflower seeds	Chocolate chips
Pine nuts	Granola
Peanuts	Dried fruit
Almonds	Cheerios
Chex cereal	Coconut
Miniature marshmallows	

- Large plastic zip-lock bag

How You Make It:

1. Measure ½ cup each of any five of the above ingredients.

2. Put all ingredients in a large plastic zip-lock bag and shake to mix.

3. Store uneaten trail mix in same plastic zip-lock bag.

OF COURSE (JUST BETWEEN YOU AND ME) REAL INDIANS DON'T USE ZIP LOCK BAGS.

40. JACK-O-LANTERN COOKIES

Materials You Need:

- Store-bought or homemade round sugar cookies
- 1 can white frosting
- Yellow and red food coloring
- Knife
- Spoon
- Candy Corn

How You Make It:

1. Add a few drops of yellow and red food coloring to white frosting and stir with spoon until it turns orange.
2. With knife, frost top side of cookies.
3. Decorate frosted cookies with Candy Corn to form eyes, nose, and mouth.
4. Raisins, sunflower seeds, nuts, etc. may be substituted for Candy Corn.

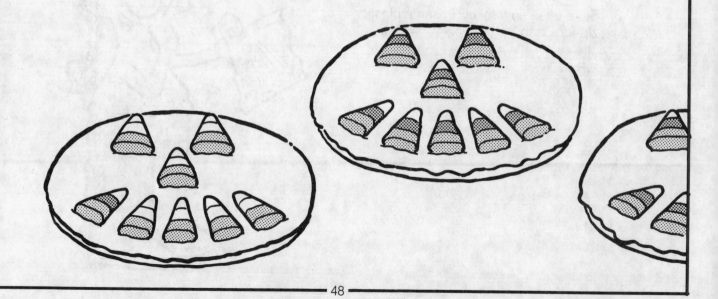

41. MONSTER MATCH

Materials You Need:

- 3" x 5" index cards
- Black marker

How You Do It:

1. Write the following words on two index cards each:

Halloween	R.I.P.	Graveyard
Witch	Boo	Spooks
Ghost	Witches Brew	Goblins
Haunted House	Monster	Spider
Skeleton	Frankenstein	Creepy Crawlers

2. Mix up index cards and lay face down on the floor. Children take turns turning over two cards, hoping to make a match. If the child makes a match, he/she gets to keep those two cards and tries again. If the child does not make a match, the game continues to the next player. The person with the most matches wins.

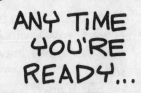

ANY TIME YOU'RE READY...

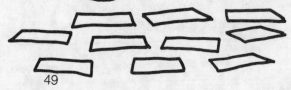

42. NATURE'S WINDOW

Materials You Need:

- Leaves
- Flower petals
- Waxed paper, 15" x 11"
- 9" x 12" piece of construction paper
- Iron *(adult supervision)*
- Tape
- Newspaper
- Scissors

How You Make It:

1. Fold waxed paper in half so the 11-inch sides meet.

2. Open the waxed paper and arrange flower petals or leaves on half of the paper, trying not to overcrowd the arrangement.

3. Refold the waxed paper. Try not to disturb the arrangement of flowers/leaves.

4. Cover the waxed paper with a piece of newspaper.

5. Have Mom or Dad press the paper-covered flowers/leaves with a warm iron. The heat will seal the flowers/leaves between the waxed paper.

6. Cut the entire center out of the construction paper, leaving a one-inch border all around to form a frame.

7. Tape the waxed paper flowers/leaves to the construction paper frame from behind.

8. Tape the nature window to your window and watch the sunlight shine through the flowers/leaves.

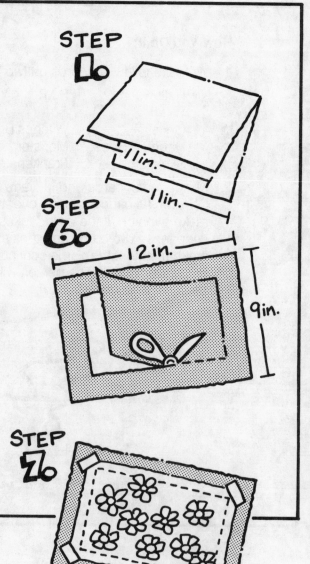

STEP 1.

STEP 6.

STEP 7.

11 in.

11 in.

12 in.

9 in.

43. PENCIL GHOSTS

Materials You Need:

- Pencil
- White napkin
- Black yarn
- Black marker
- Small styrofoam ball

How You Make It:

1. Poke a styrofoam ball onto the eraser end of a pencil.
2. Cover the styrofoam ball with a napkin and secure it with a piece of black yarn tied in a bow.
3. With black marker, make two black eyes.

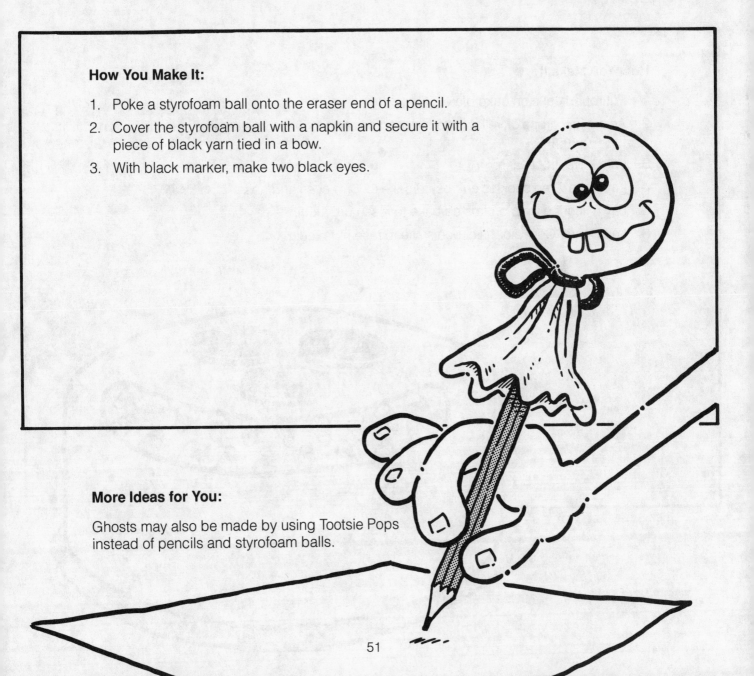

More Ideas for You:

Ghosts may also be made by using Tootsie Pops instead of pencils and styrofoam balls.

44. PUMPKIN CAKE

Materials You Need:

- 1 baked round cake
- 1 can white frosting
- Yellow and red food coloring
- Cake plate
- Knife
- Spoon
- Candy Corn
- 1 licorice whip (red or black)
- 3 Oreo cookies

How You Make It:

1. Put round cake on cake plate.
2. Add a few drops of yellow and red food coloring to white frosting and stir with spoon until it turns orange.
3. With knife, frost cake.
4. Lay three Oreo cookies on frosted cake to form eyes and nose.
5. Lay a licorice whip on frosted cake to resemble mouth.
6. Lay Candy Corn along licorice smile to resemble teeth.

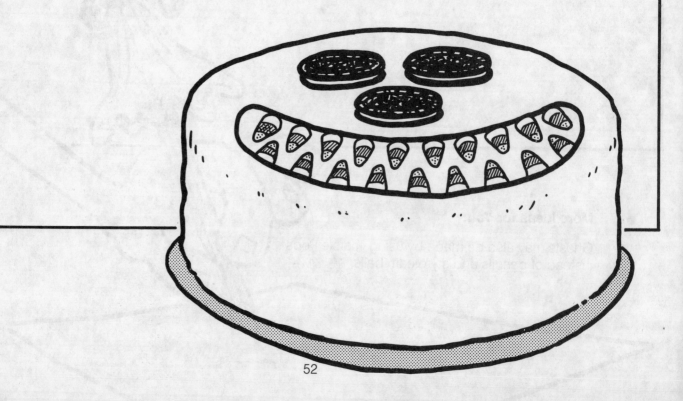

45. PUMPKIN MATCH

Materials You Need:

- Orange construction paper
- Scissors
- Pencil
- Pumpkin cookie cutter (large size)

How You Do It:

1. Trace several pumpkin cookie cutter shapes onto orange construction paper. Cut out.
2. Cut each pumpkin in half differently. See illustration.
3. Mix up pumpkin halves.
4. Pass out a pumpkin half to each child.
5. Have children find their pumpkin match.

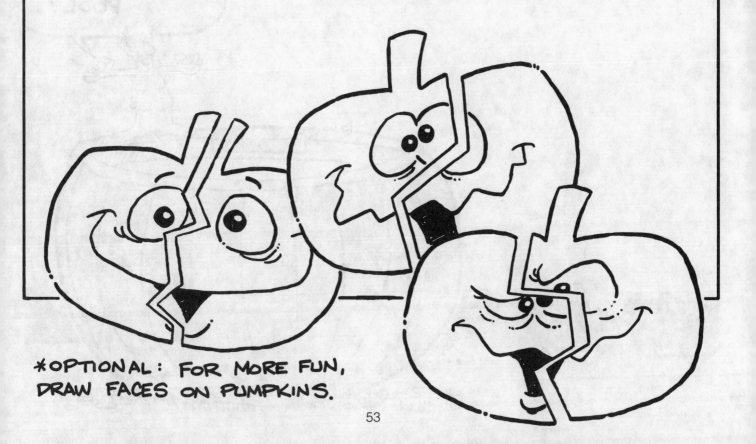

*OPTIONAL: FOR MORE FUN, DRAW FACES ON PUMPKINS.

46. PUMPKIN VASE

Materials You Need:

- Pumpkin
- Pumpkin cutter
- Spoon
- Newspaper
- Flowers
- Water

How You Make It:

1. Cover work area with newspaper.
2. Cut top off pumpkin with pumpkin cutter.
3. Clean out inside of pumpkin with spoon.
4. Fill pumpkin half full with water.
5. Insert fresh flowers into pumpkin vase.

...AND IF YOU CAN FIND A REALLY BIG PUMPKIN, YOU CAN MAKE AN AFFORDABLE BACK YARD POOL!

47. SPIDER CUPCAKES

Materials You Need:

- Baked cupcakes
- 1 can chocolate frosting
- Knife
- Licorice whips (black)
- Black gumdrops

How You Make It:

1. With knife, frost cupcakes with chocolate frosting.
2. Cut licorice whips into three-inch pieces.
3. Poke licorice whips in sides of cupcake for legs.
4. Attach two black gumdrops on top of cupcakes for eyes.

48. SPOOKY FILL-IN

Materials You Need:

- Pencil
- "Spooky Fill-In" puzzle

How You Do It:

From the clues given below, fill in the puzzle squares. Answers on page 125.

3 letters:
RIP
CAT
BAT

5 letters:
WITCH
GHOST
CANDY
BROOM

6 letters:
TRICKS
TREATS
SPIDER

7 letters:
PUMPKIN
MONSTER

8 letters:
COSTUMES

12 letters:
HAUNTED HAUSE
JACK O LANTERN

49. STYRO SPIDER

Materials You Need:

- 6-inch styrofoam ball
- 8 black pipe cleaners
- Knife
- Black acrylic paint
- Beaded eyes
- Glue
- Paint brush

How You Make It:

1. Cut styrofoam ball in half.

2. Paint ball half with black acrylic paint. Let dry.

3. Lay ball flat side down to form spider body.

4. Attach four pipe cleaners on each side of body by poking pipe cleaners into styrofoam ball.

5. Bend legs to make spider look like he's walking.

6. Glue two beaded eyes in place. Let dry.

More Ideas for You:

Small spiders may be made by using smaller styrofoam balls and by cutting pipe cleaners in half.

50₀ SWEET POTATO VINE

Materials You Need:

- Mayonnaise jar
- Water
- Sweet potato
- 4 toothpicks

How You Make It:

1. Fill jar with water.

2. Insert four toothpicks around middle of sweet potato.

3. Set the sweet potato on the jar so the end of the potato is in the water. Be sure to keep enough water in the jar so the end of the potato is always covered.

4. Set in a sunny location.

5. After a few weeks you will see a vine beginning to grow.

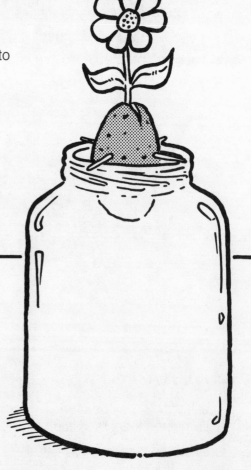

NOTE FROM THE ARTIST: NOT ONLY IS THIS A NIFTY PROJECT, BUT YOU CAN ALSO USE THIS ILLUSTRATION TO PLAY "WHAT'S WRONG WITH THIS PICTURE?"

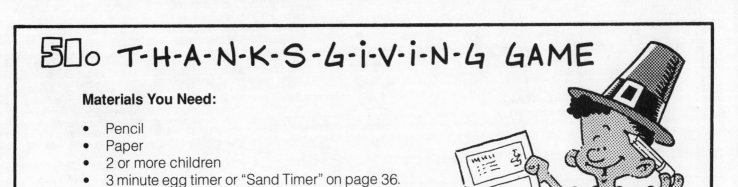

5o T·H·A·N·K·S·G·i·V·i·N·G GAME

Materials You Need:

- Pencil
- Paper
- 2 or more children
- 3 minute egg timer or "Sand Timer" on page 36.

How You Do It:

1. Give each child a pencil and a piece of paper.
2. Set the egg timer for three minutes, or turn over the "Sand Timer."
3. Each child writes as many words using the letters in *thanksgiving* as they can find.
4. At the end of three minutes, score the words by giving one point for each letter.
5. The child with the highest score is the winner.

More Ideas for You:

This game can be played by using any holiday or title.

WHA' DA YA MEAN "GATSHNIVIK" AIN'T A WORD? ...IT MEANS TO FRUSTRATE LITTLE KIDS! ...I'M SICK OF THIS DOPEY GAME!! ...I'M GOING HOME...WHO BOUGHT THIS STUPID BOOK ANYWAY? I'LL BET SOME-BODY WEIRD MADE UP ALL THESE GOOFY GAMES! I'VE HAD IT UP TO HERE WITH THIS ......

52. TOTEM POLE

Materials You Need:

- 5 large-size thread spools
- Glue
- Acrylic paint—assorted colors
- Paint brush
- Styrofoam cup with water for cleaning paint brush

How You Make It:

1. Paint spools with colors of your choice. Let dry.
2. Paint a different face on each spool. Let dry.
3. Glue spools on top of one another. Let dry.

FOR EXTRA CREDIT, USE CONSTRUCTION PAPER TO MAKE WINGS AND A FEATHER FOR THE TOP.

More Ideas for You:

Feathers and paper wings may be glued in place for added effect.

HOW COME I'M ALWAYS ON THE BOTTOM?

53. TURKEY TROT

Materials You Need:

- Chairs
- Friends

How You Do It:

1. All but one child sits in a circle on chairs.

2. One child stands in the center of the circle.

3. Every child gets a title of "cranberries," "stuffing," or "pumpkin pie." For
   example: Child #1 is "cranberries"
   Child #2 is "stuffing"
   Child #3 is "pumpkin pie"

4. The titles then start over: Child #4 is "cranberries"
   Child #5 is "stuffing"
   Child #6 is "pumpkin pie"

   and so on.

5. When all the children have a title the game may begin.

6. The child in the center of the circle calls out one of the titles other than his/her
   own.

7. Everyone with that title must stand up and switch places with each other.

8. The child in the center tries to sit in one of the chairs before the others switch.

9. The person without a chair goes to the center of the circle and calls out a
   different title and the race is on again.

10. If the child in the center chooses to upset the game, he/she calls out "Turkey
    Trot" instead of one of the other titles.

11. Everyone must then change places.

12. The last person standing again becomes the caller, choosing to call a title or
    "Turkey Trot."

13. Remember, every time someone in the center calls out "Turkey Trot" *everyone*
    must change places.

More Ideas for You:

This game may be played for any holiday by changing the titles.

54o WALNUT MOUSE

Materials You Need:

- ½ walnut shell
- 1 marble
- 1 piece of string about 2 inches long
- 2 small wiggly eyes from craft store
- Small piece of black construction paper
- Scissors
- Glue

How You Make It:

1. Place ½ walnut shell upside down over a marble.

2. Glue the piece of string to one end of the shell to form a tail. Let dry.

3. Glue the wiggly eyes in place on the other end of the shell. Let dry.

4. Cut two small triangles from the construction paper. Fold each triangle in half lengthwise.

5. Glue the triangles onto the top of the shell to form ears. Let dry.

6. Now give your mouse a gentle push and watch him scurry across the floor.

WiNTER

Calico Heart
Chocolate Covered Pretzels
Favorite Collage
Hanukkah Greeting Card
Hanukkah Spelling Game
Holiday Search
Log Cabin
Menorah Snack
Presidential Top Secret
Secret Word
Spell-A-Holiday
Valentine Card Holder
Valentine Puzzle
Wintery Salt-Paint Scene
Year Book

55. CALICO HEART

Materials You Need:

- Thin coat hanger
- About sixty 6" x $1\frac{1}{2}$" strips of fabric (cotton/poly blends) in assorted colors
- Scissors

How You Make It:

1. Bend the coat hanger into a heart shape.
2. Tie fabric strips in a knot around the hanger.
3. Hang on your wall as a cute country decoration.

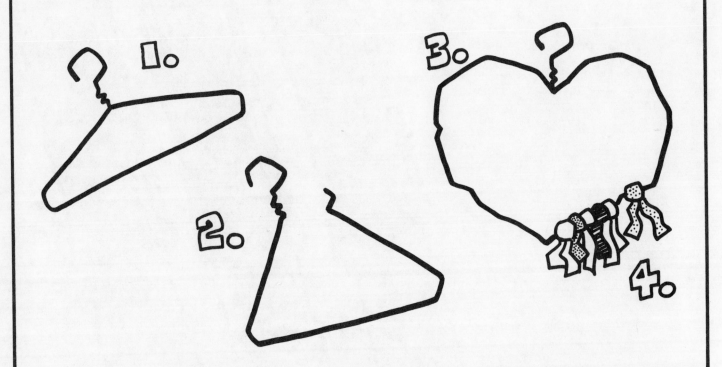

56. CHOCOLATE COVERED PRETZELS

Materials You Need:

- 1 bag pretzels, sticks or twisted
- 1 package white chocolate or milk chocolate chips
- Aluminum foil
- Bowl
- Spoon
- Microwave oven

How You Make It:

1. Lay a sheet of aluminum foil on the table.

2. Pour chocolate chips in a bowl.

3. Melt chocolate in the microwave oven. Stir until smooth and soft.

4. Dip half a pretzel in the chocolate and lay it on the aluminum foil.

5. Continue dipping pretzels until chocolate is gone.

6. Let the chocolate-dipped pretzels harden about 30 minutes to 1 hour, depending on how much chocolate is on the pretzel.

7. Remove from aluminum foil.

8. Eat and enjoy.

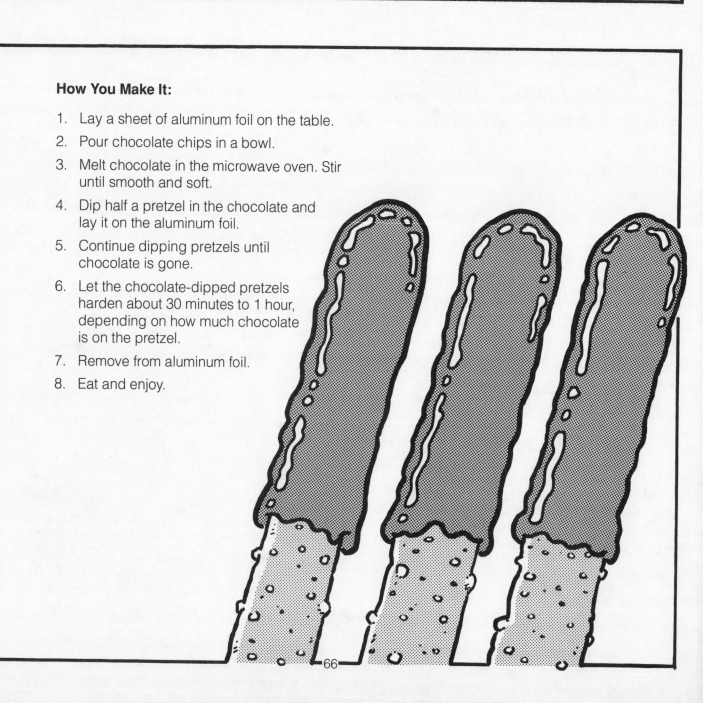

57o FAVORITE COLLAGE

Materials You Need:

- 8½" x 11" sheet of red construction paper
- Scissors
- Glue
- Magazines

How You Make It:

1. Cut out a large heart from the red construction paper.

2. Cut out pictures of your favorite foods, hobbies, clothes, etc. from magazines.

3. Glue your favorite pictures to your heart. Let dry.

THIS IS MY FAVORITE THING!

CHOCOLATE NET WT. 2Z

58. HANUKKAH GREETING CARD

Materials You Need:

- Colored construction paper
- Colored yarn
- Glue
- Felt-tip pen

How You Make It:

1. Fold the construction paper in half to form a card.
2. Carefully drizzle glue on the cover of the card to form a Star of David.
3. Cover the glue with yarn and let dry.
4. Write your Hanukkah message on the inside of the card.

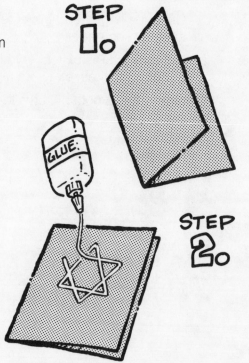

STEP 1.

STEP 2.

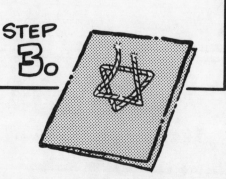

STEP 3.

59. HANUKKAH SPELLING GAME

Materials You Need:

- Construction paper
- Scissors
- Felt-tip pen
- Glue

How You Do It:

1. Cut out 16 small triangles for *every two* children who expect to play.

2. Glue the triangles together to form eight Stars of David (see illustration). Let dry.

3. Print one letter from the word "Hanukkah" on each star.

4. Mix up the stars.

5. Divide the children into two's.

6. Every two children receives eight stars.

7. The game is played by having the children trade their stars to form the word "Hanukkah."

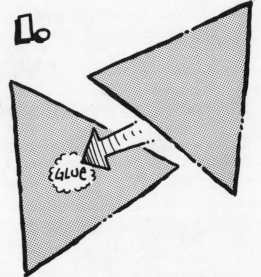

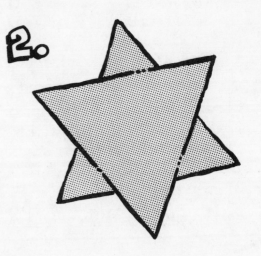

60. HOLIDAY SEARCH

Materials You Need:

- Pencil
- "Holiday Search" game

How You Do It:

Find the holidays listed below and draw a line around them. Answers may be horizontal, vertical, or diagonal. Answers are on page 125.

Christmas
Chinese New Year
Mother's Day
Father's Day
Hanukkah
American Indian Day
Easter
Halloween
Thanksgiving
St. Patrick's Day
Last Day of School
Back to School
Fourth of July
New Year's Day
Valentine's Day
Birthday

```
S L L M O T H A B E A O V D A Y F
T A S O B A C K T O S C H O O L O
M S C T G H I A N T T H D A Y V U
A T R H L L O W W E Y H H R S A R
S D A E R D A Y O A S C A V T L T
O A D R F I S H D A Y S L X S E H
R Y O S I O S H I N E T L E T N O
V O Y D R P T T A U R E O S P T F
O F R A S R P A M K T R W E T I J
T S A Y I T A N E A S T E R H N U
R C O B T V T K R H S M E I A E L
C H R A X W R G I I A A N C N S Y
B O B K F G I V C T R S P A K D W
T O D I H D C N A H U N K N S A E
F L A T Q U K G N E M G P S G Y E
A I Y S R F S P I R O V W T I E S
T A N C V I D T N S M Q U O V T N
H A N U K K A H D A S N U F I E E
E S U L O L Y D I Y I E E S N R W
R T K L L U E D A D L U N C G S T
S C H I N E S E N E W Y E A R A H
D H A M K R T M D O O E A O E U O
A U H N S D E N A G W A R O N H F
Y R I C A N E W Y E A R S D A Y J
```

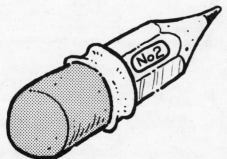

60 LOG CABIN

Materials You Need:

- 1 bag of pretzel sticks
- 2 sheets of brown construction paper
- Scissors
- Powdered sugar (optional)

How You Do It:

1. Lay a piece of brown construction paper on the table.

2. Lay two pretzel sticks vertically parallel with each other.

3. Lay two more pretzel sticks horizontally parallel on top of the first two.

4. Continue to alternate pretzel sticks until cabin is as tall as you want, being careful not to build it so tall that it falls over.

5. Cut a piece of construction paper about twice as big as the log cabin.

6. Fold the paper in half.

7. Open the paper and set it on top of the cabin to form a roof.

8. While making the cabin, talk about what you think it would have been like to live in the pioneer days.

9. For a winter log cabin, sprinkle powdered sugar over the roof to resemble snow.

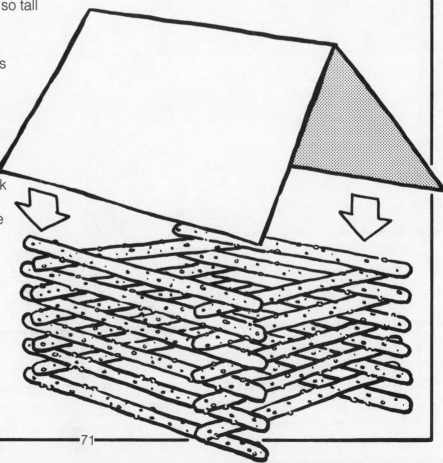

62. MENORAH SNACK

Materials You Need:

- 1 slice of bread
- Peanut butter
- 8 sunflower nuts
- 8 pretzel sticks
- 1 carrot or celery stick

How You Make It:

1. Spread a slice of bread with peanut butter.
2. Arrange one large carrot or celery stick in center of bread on top of peanut butter to form a large candle.
3. Arrange four pretzel sticks as candles on each side of the large candle.
4. Attach sunflower nuts as flames.
5. Enjoy. Yum, yum.

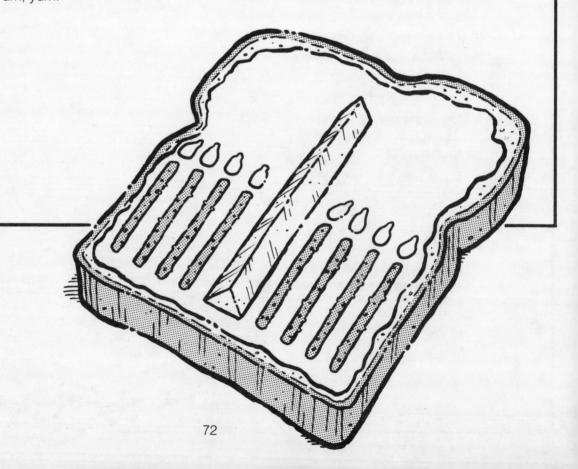

63. PRESIDENTIAL TOP SECRET

Materials You Need:

- Pencil
- "Presidential Top Secret" game

How You Do It:

1. Unscramble the Presidents' names.
2. When all Presidents are unscrambled, place the letters from the star spaces into the "secret word" square to reveal the secret word. Answers on page 126.

STNGWIAHNO

OISMDNA

NDENYEK

GNRAAE

IOLLNCN

TRCRAE

RNTMUA

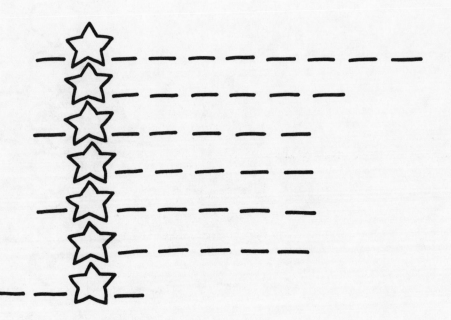

64o SECRET WORD

Materials You Need:

- Pencil
- "Secret Word" game

How You Do It:

From the clues below, fill in the answers and when you've finished you'll know the "secret word." Answers on page 126. Clues:

1. Special
2. Valentine Shape
3. Feeling
4. Color
5. Sweets
6. Loving Person
7. Smack
8. Gift
9. Blossoms

65. SPELL-A-HOLIDAY

Materials You Need:

- 3" x 5" index cards
- Felt-tip pen
- 6 or more children
- 8 or more envelopes

How You Do It:

1. Choose eight or more holiday names.

2. Print each letter of a holiday name on a 3" by 5" index card.

3. When the holiday is spelled out, mix up the letters and put them in an envelope.

4. Repeat this procedure until you have eight or more envelopes filled with the letters of individual holidays.

5. Choose two or more teams.

6. Give each team an envelope.

7. At a signal, have the teams open their envelope.

8. The team members sort out the letters to form the name of their holiday correctly.

9. See which team can spell the word first.

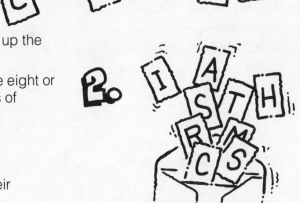

GEE, I'VE NEVER CELEBRATED "THRASMICS!"

66. VALENTINE CARD HOLDER

Materials You Need:

- 2 large paper plates
- 2 pieces of yarn each 2 yards long (colors of your choice)
- Scissors
- Single-hole paper punch
- Crayons or colored pens

How You Make It:

1. Cut one paper plate according to the illustration.
2. Place cut paper plate on top of whole plate to form a pocket.
3. With plates together, punch holes at one-inch intervals.
4. Thread both pieces of yarn through holes leaving a generous length of yarn on each end to tie together to form a hanger.
5. Decorate the top plate with crayons or colored pens.

67. VALENTINE PUZZLE

Materials You Need:

- 8½" x 11" sheet of red construction paper
- Scissors
- Large envelope

How You Make It:

1. Cut a large valentine from red construction paper.
2. Cut the valentine into 12 pieces.
3. Mix up the valentine pieces and put into the envelope.
4. Give the valentine to a friend.
5. The friend removes the puzzle pieces from the envelope and recreates your valentine.

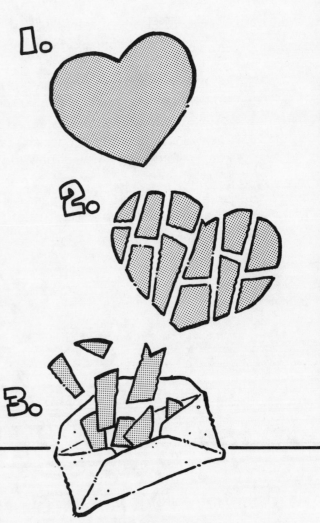

More Ideas for You:

Write a message on the valentine before you begin cutting the puzzle design.

68. WINTERY SALT-PAINT SCENE

Materials You Need:

- 2 teaspoons salt per color
- 1 teaspoon liquid starch per color
- 1 teaspoon water per color
- Spoon
- Tempera paint (different colors)
- Paint brush
- Paper
- Pencil
- Small container (yogurt containers work great)
- Styrofoam cup with water
- Napkin

How You Make It:

1. Draw a winter scene on paper with pencil.

2. Mix salt, liquid starch, and water in small container with spoon. Add a few drops of tempera paint. Mix well.

3. Mix one recipe of salt, liquid starch, and water per container. Add a few drops of tempera paint to create different colors. Be sure to keep one container of white paint.

4. Paint your picture with salt paint. Clean paint brush in cup of water before using a new color. Wipe off excess water on napkin.

5. Let dry. When dry, the white paint will look like snow and the other colors will have an "icy" effect.

78

69. YEAR BOOK

Materials You Need:

- 3-ring binder
- 12 index cards
- Binder paper
- Crayons, colored pencils, or felt-tip markers
- Fashion magazines
- Newspaper articles
- Number stickers
- Scissors
- Glue

How You Make It:

1. Label each index tab with a different month.

2. Insert index tabs onto sheets of binder paper.

3. With crayons, colored pencils, or felt-tip markers, create a cover picture on each index page. For example: December may have a Christmas tree; February may have a heart; September may have a school house, etc.

4. Insert index pages into three-ring binder.

5. Add empty sheets of binder paper between index pages.

6. To the front of the binder, attach number stickers announcing which year the year book will represent.

7. As frequently as possible, add bits of information to your year book. For example: write what you did today; cut out newspaper articles or fashion pictures from magazines and glue in your year book; have friends autograph your year book; write about your vacation or some special event, etc.

CHRISTMAS

Advent Wreath

Angel Gift Bag

Beaded Candy Cane

Button Tree

Candy-Candy Cane

Christmas Candle Holder

Christmas Candle Salad

Christmas Craf-tivity Calendar

Christmas Crossword Puzzle

Christmas Place Mats

Christmas Play—"Twas the Week before Christmas"

Christmas Tree Puppet

Clay Ornaments—No Bake Method

E-Z Eggnog Punch

Gift Tags

Gingerbread Man Ornament

Glitter Stencil Gift Wrap

Jewelry Tree

Macaroni Garland

Macaroni Snowflake

Miniature Christmas Tree Garland

Paper Christmas Ornament

Plastic Lacey Ornament

Santa Gift Bag

Shiny Spirals

Silver Bells

Soapy Ornament

Soapy Snowman Sculpture

Stocking Sewing Cards

Straw Burst Decoration

Sweet 'n Spicy Pomander

70₀ ADVENT WREATH

Materials You Need:

- 2 potatoes
- Aluminum foil
- Plate
- Knife/Spoon
- Artificial Christmas greenery or holly
- 4 candles

How You Make It:

1. Cut two potatoes in half. Lay potato halves flat side down.

2. Scoop out a hole in each potato half for a candle to fit. Insert candle.

3. Cover potato with aluminum foil.

4. Arrange the potato/candles on a plate and lay Christmas greenery or holly around candles.

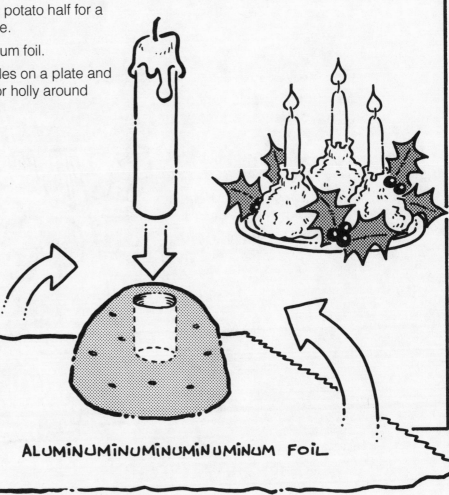

ALUMINUMINUMINUMINUMINUM FOIL

7⬜o ANGEL GIFT BAG

Materials You Need:

- White shopping bag with handles
- Yellow yarn
- Red, blue, and pink construction paper
- Gold rick-rack
- Gold ribbon
- 1 large round paper lace doily
- Scissors
- Adhesive tape
- Glue

How You Make It:

1. Open shopping bag. Insert gift. Tape top of bag shut.

2. Cut two circles from blue construction paper for eyes and glue in place. Let dry.

3. Cut two large circles from pink construction paper for cheeks and glue in place. Let dry.

4. Cut a smile shape from red construction paper and glue in place. Let dry.

5. Glue gold rick-rack to form neckline of angel. Let dry.

6. Tie a bow from gold ribbon and glue at center of neckline. Let dry.

7. Cut yellow yarn in pieces and glue in place for hair. Let dry.

8. Cut large round paper doily in half. Fold doily halves in half.

9. Tape folded doily halves to sides of bag to form wings (see illustration).

73. BEADED CANDY CANE

Materials You Need:

- White or silver pipe cleaners
- Clear and red plastic beads with center opening as large as pipe cleaner diameter

How You Make It:

1. Alternating colors, string beads on pipe cleaner.
2. Fold ends of pipe cleaner over first and last bead to secure.
3. Bend beaded pipe cleaner to form candy cane shape.
4. Attach a short piece of pipe cleaner at bend of candy cane to form hanger.

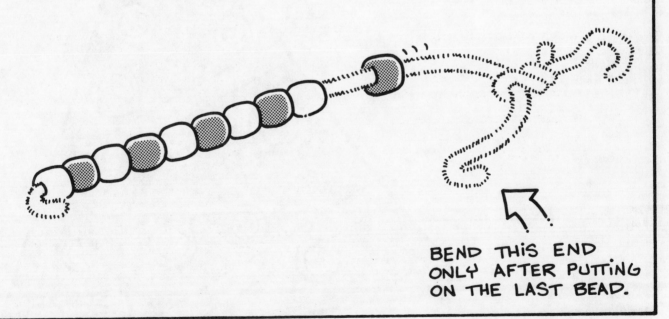

BEND THIS END ONLY AFTER PUTTING ON THE LAST BEAD.

NOTE: YOU CAN USE ANY SHAPE OF BEAD...ROUND ONES ARE JUST EASIER FOR ME TO DRAW. - THE ILLUSTRATOR

73. BUTTON TREE

Materials You Need:

- 9" x 12" piece of green posterboard
- Scissors
- Buttons of assorted shapes, sizes, and colors
- Tacky glue
- Ribbon
- Adhesive tape

How You Make It:

1. Cut a triangle shape from posterboard with scissors.

2. Wrap ribbon around tree to form garland and tape to back.

3. Glue assorted buttons to tree for decorations.

4. Glue a large, bright button to top of tree in place of star.

5. Let dry.

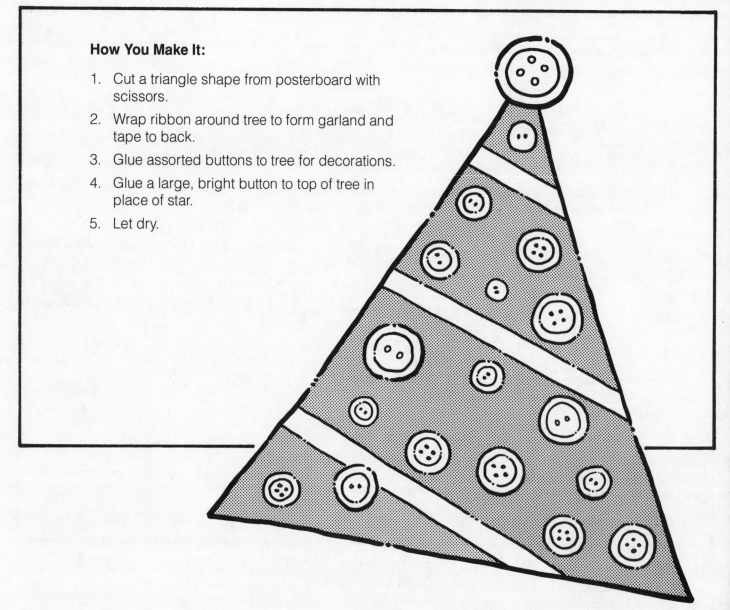

74. CANDY-CANDY CANE

Materials You Need:

- Medium to large size candy cane (individually wrapped)
- 6-inch square of nylon netting
- Brightly colored ribbon
- Scissors
- Candy pieces (M&M's, Hershey Kisses, hard Christmas candy, etc.)
- Plastic wrap (optional)

How You Make It:

1. If candy pieces are not individually wrapped, wrap in a small piece of plastic wrap.

2. Place the wrapped candy in center of square of nylon netting.

3. Pull sides of netting up and tie tightly with brightly colored ribbon.

4. Attach candy bag to candy cane with same ribbon.

5. Finish with a bright bow.

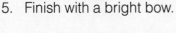

More Ideas for You:

"Candy-Candy Canes" may be used as a decoration on top of a gift, holiday fruit basket, or nut bread. Smaller versions of the "Candy-Candy Canes" may be used as favors for children's parties or friends visiting during the holidays.

75. CHRISTMAS CANDLE HOLDER

Materials You Need:

- Lid from spray can that has a circular rim inside
- Rick-rack, lace, braid, or any fabric trim
- White glue
- Scissors
- Candle

How You Make It:

1. Cut pieces of fabric trim of your choice long enough to go around the spray can lid.

2. Glue trim to lid. Let dry.

3. Insert candle in center of lid.

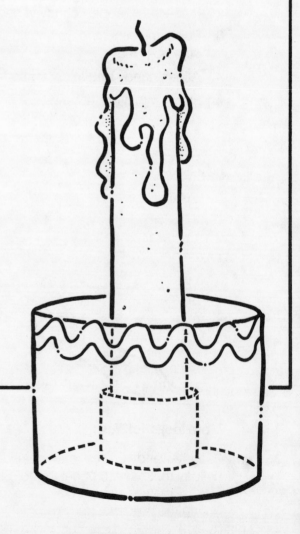

76. CHRISTMAS CANDLE SALAD

Materials You Need:

- ½ banana
- 1 canned pineapple ring
- 1 lettuce leaf (washed)
- 1 cherry
- 1 spoonful of whipping cream
- Salad plate

How You Make It:

1. Place a lettuce leaf on a salad plate.
2. Lay a pineapple ring on the lettuce leaf.
3. Stand a banana half upright in center of the pineapple ring.
4. Drop a spoonful of whipping cream on top of the banana and let it run down the sides.
5. Put cherry on top of banana (makes one serving).

77. CHRISTMAS CRAF-TIVITY CALENDAR

Materials You Need:

- Pencil or crayons
- Blank calendar on following page

How You Make It:

1. Label and number days on blank calendar.
2. Look through *YOU CAN MAKE IT! YOU CAN DO IT!* book.
3. Select a craf-tivity for each day and write its title in the calendar days.
4. Hang the calendar where you can create your selected craf-tivity every day for the month of December.

More Ideas for You:

Calendar may be made for any month.

CRAF-TIVITY CALENDAR

SUN	MON	TUE	WED	THUR	FRI	SAT

78. CHRISTMAS CROSSWORD PUZZLE

Materials You Need:

- Pencil
- "Christmas Crossword Puzzle"

How You Do It:

Read the clues below and fill in the answers on the crossword puzzle. Thanks to all the special people from Gomes Elementary School for these crafty crossword clues. Answers on page 126.

1. A fat, jolly man dressed in a red suit that lives at the North Pole; Worker at North Pole; Jolly man who celebrates Christmas; Kris Kringle; St. Nick.
2. Powder puff; A white wonder, fabulous, fluffy, frosty flakes; White icy powder; White blanket covering the floor.
3. Christmas candy; A colorful striped delicious treat for Christmas *(2 words)*.
4. Small fire; Burns brightly; Bright light; A warm glowing light when all else is dark; Comforting, relaxing, delighting.
5. Secret golden star; Something decorating the Christmas tree; Beautiful design on a Christmas tree.
6. Ring of Christmas decoration.
7. Christmas singers; Singers at night, singing in the snow.
8. Leader of the pack.
9. Munchkin small enough to eat; A gnome who works for Santa.
10. Winter tales.
11. White and cold, just like crystal.
12. Evergreen tree; Christmas monument; Something you decorate before Christmas.
13. A red-nosed animal.
14. A greedy man.
15. Sparkling ornaments covering the house and all the rooms.
16. Chocolate chip treats; Small baked thing: Yummy, yummy, good for tummy.
17. A white, sparkling, jolly old man.
18. *(across)* A dancing light or a blaze.
19. *(down)* Snowman.
20. The source of the original Christmas story.
21. Hung on the mantle near a sparkling fire.
22. Juicy, sticky peppermint.

79. CHRISTMAS PLACE MATS

Materials You Need:

- Old Christmas cards
- Piece of construction paper approximately 12" x 18"
- Glue
- Scissors
- Clear plastic laminate (can be purchased wherever shelf paper is sold)

How You Make It:

1. Glue old Christmas cards to construction paper being sure to overlap cards slightly and form a collage. Let dry.

2. Cover entire placemat (both sides) with a sheet of clear plastic laminate. (Applying plastic laminate can be tricky as it sometimes wrinkles. You may need some adult supervision with this.)

3. If plastic laminate extends over edges of collage, trim with scissors.

WHEN CUTTING THE EXCESS LAMINATE FROM THE PLACE MAT, LEAVE A 1/4 INCH EDGE FROM EDGE OF PLACE MAT.

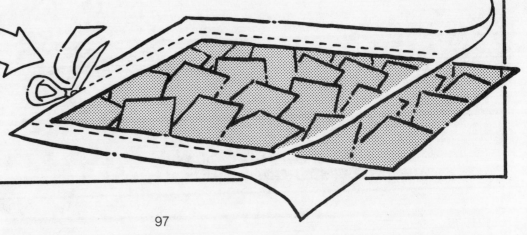

80. CHRISTMAS TREE PUPPET

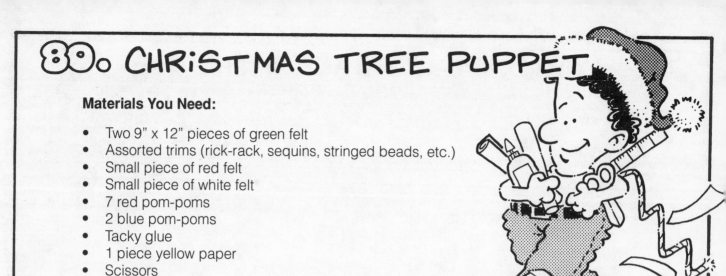

Materials You Need:

- Two 9" x 12" pieces of green felt
- Assorted trims (rick-rack, sequins, stringed beads, etc.)
- Small piece of red felt
- Small piece of white felt
- 7 red pom-poms
- 2 blue pom-poms
- Tacky glue
- 1 piece yellow paper
- Scissors
- Pencil

How You Make It:

1. Cut one large Christmas tree from one 9" by 12" piece of green felt.
2. Lay Christmas tree on second piece of green felt and trace.
3. Cut second tree same size as first tree.
4. Put glue along side and top edges of one tree. Do not glue bottom edge. Cover with second tree and press edges together. Let dry.
5. Cut two circles from white felt and glue in place for eyes.
6. Cut two circles from red felt and glue in place for cheeks.
7. Cut one smile from red felt and glue in place.
8. Glue one red pom-pom in place for nose.
9. Glue two blue pom-poms in center of white felt eyes.
10. Glue red pom-poms to edges of tree.
11. Glue on sequins/trim decoration.
12. Cut a star from yellow paper and glue to top of tree.
13. Let dry.

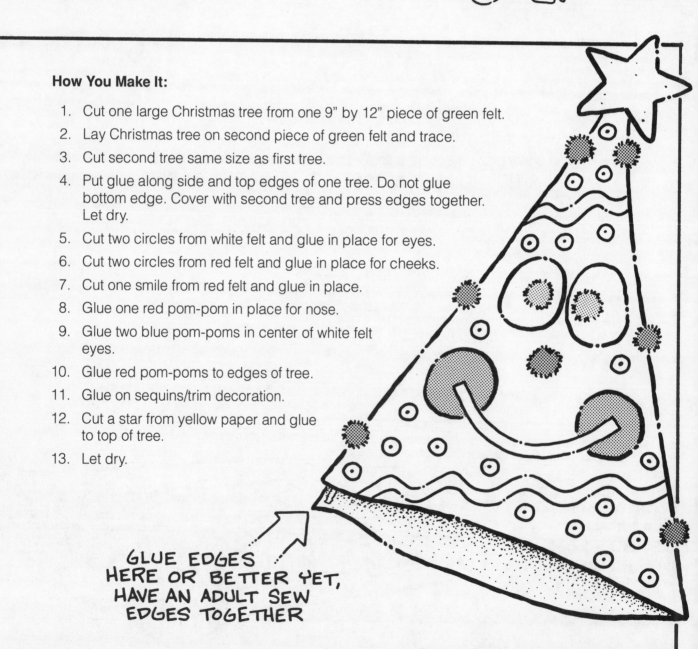

GLUE EDGES HERE OR BETTER YET, HAVE AN ADULT SEW EDGES TOGETHER

81. CHRISTMAS PLAY: TWAS THE WEEK BEFORE CHRISTMAS BY JULLIEN KILLE

Materials You Need:

Cast:
- Carolers
- Holliday family—five members
- Frosty the Snowman
- Seven friends
- Santa

Props:
- Desk with chair
- Table
- Decorated Christmas tree with presents
- Cardboard fireplace
- Rocking chair
- Window frame
- Door frame
- Large cardboard snowman
- Large cardboard sleigh
- Hat for Frosty the Snowman
- Jingle bells for carolers
- Cookies

Cont'd.

Materials You Need *Cont'd.*

Costumes:
- Colorful sweatshirts or sweaters and pants
- Mittens
- Hats
- Scarves
- Angel costume
- Two shepherd costumes
- Three king costumes with crowns and gifts
- Mary and Joseph robes (doll for Baby Jesus)
- Velvet bow ties for carolers
- White shirts/blouses for carolers
- Dark pants/skirts for carolers

Songs:
- "We Wish You a Merry Christmas"
- "Jingle Bells"
- "It's Beginning to Look a Lot like Christmas"
- "Let It Snow, Let It Snow, Let It Snow"
- "Frosty the Snowman"
- "Sleigh Ride"
- "Have Yourself a Merry Little Christmas"
- "Rockin' around the Christmas Tree"
- "O Little Town of Bethlehem"
- "It Came upon a Midnight Clear"
- "Silent Night"
- "Silver Bells"

How You Do It:

ACT I (curtain opens)

Scene 1: Twas the week before Christmas, when all thru the house
The Holliday family was busy as a mouse.
The stockings were hung by the chimney with care
In hopes that St. Nicholas soon would be there.

Scene 2: Dad paid the bills from Mervyn's and Macy's
While Mom wrapped presents for Tammy, Sue, and Stacey.
The girls hung the holly around the front door
While Tammy dreamed of toys and presents galore.

Scene 3: When down the street there arose such a clatter
The family ran to see what was the matter.
Away to the door they stood with a smile
To find [?#] carolers arriving single file.

Scene 4: They took their form while jingle bells rang
"We Wish You a Merry Christmas" is the song that they sang.

Scene 5: The Holliday family asked for an encore
So the carolers sang just two more.

Scene 6:   The children grew sleepy so went on to bed
             With visions of snowfall dancing in their heads.
             The moon shone brightly on the new fallen snow
             As the children dreamed on, "Let It Snow, Let It Snow, Let It Snow."

(curtain closes)

ACT II   *(curtain opens)*

Scene 1:   Morning time came and the children's dreams
             Were fulfilled with snow that was supreme.
             They ran out of doors for they had a great plan
             To build the happiest and liveliest snowman.

Scene 2:   *(No narration. See Scene Description.)*

Scene 3:   The season is merry with joy everywhere
             So family and friends shared in Holliday cheer.
             There were cookies and cocoa and presents to share.
             It was the happiest season anywhere.

Scene 4:   *(No narration. See Scene Description.)*

Scene 5:   The party was grand with joy all around
             Then Mom told a story as the children sat down
             Of another Christmas long, long ago
             Of another family and a child that was born.
             The music tells the sweet and pleasant story
             Of how this child came to share His glory.
             In a little manger where He lay
             Love and peace were born that day.

(curtain closes)

ACT III   *(No narration. See Scene Description.)*

Scene 1:   "O Little Town of Bethlehem"

Scene 2:   "It Came upon a Midnight Clear"

Scene 3:   "Silent Night"

ACT IV   *(curtain opens) (No narration. See Scene Description.)*

Scene 1:   "Silver Bells"

More Ideas for You:

Scene Description: Story is narrated. There are no "speaking parts" on stage. All scenes are done in "mime" form.

ACT I

Curtain opens. We see five people (Holliday family), a desk and chair, table, Christmas tree, fireplace, rocking chair, presents under the tree, a door and window frame.

Scene 1: The Holliday family is preparing for Christmas.

Scene 2: Dad sits by a desk paying bills.
Mom stands by a table wrapping presents.
Sue and Stacey are hanging holly around the front door.
Tammy lays on the floor near the Christmas tree, daydreaming.

Scene 3: Family runs to door and looks out into audience. From back of auditorium enter carolers ringing jingle bells.

Scene 4: Carolers arrange themselves at bottom of stage on risers, forming a Christmas tree pattern. The smallest caroler is on top row wearing a star on his/her head. All other carolers wear green or red velvet bow ties on white shirts. the green bow ties represent the Christmas tree, and the red ones, the ornaments. The carolers sing "We Wish You a Merry Christmas."

Scene 5: The Holliday family applaud and motion with their hands to sing some more. The carolers sing "Jingle Bells" and "It's Beginning to Look a Lot like Christmas."

Scene 6: The children yawn and rub their eyes and the entire Holliday family slowly exit stage. Curtain closes. While the family is sleeping, the carolers sing "Let It Snow, Let It Snow, Let It Snow."

ACT II *(curtain opens)*

Scene 1: Center stage displays a large cardboard snowman with no hat. His hat lays on the floor. The Holliday children enter the living room and run to the front door to get their mittens, hats, and scarves. They dress themselves and run outside to the snowman. The carolers sing "Frosty the Snowman" as the children pretend to be playing in the snow. At the words, "there must have been some magic in that old silk hat they found for when they placed it on his head," one of the children picks up the hat and puts it to the head of the cardboard snowman. A real live Frosty takes the hat and dances out from behind the cardboard snowman. The remaining song is danced by Frosty and the three Holliday children. At the end of the song the children and Frosty skip off stage taking the cardboard snowman with them.

Scene 2: Carolers sing "Sleigh Ride" and the Holliday children, Frosty, and seven friends enter the stage prancing as horses. They are pulling a cardboard sleigh which carries Mr. and Mrs. Holliday. The children dance throughout the song and exit with Mr. and Mrs. Holliday and the sleigh at the end of the song. (All characters are wearing mittens, hats, and scarves.)

Scene 3:   Everyone enters the living room and removes their mittens, hats, and scarves. The children sit around the Christmas tree as Mom passes out cookies and Dad passes out presents. The carolers sing "Have Yourself a Merry Little Christmas." While the carolers sing, the children open their presents which are actually shoe boxes (lids and bottoms gift-wrapped separately) containing tap shoes. They quietly put on their tap shoes and return their regular shoes to the gift-wrapped boxes.

Scene 4:   When the carolers finish their song, the children rise and form a single line. The carolers sing "Rockin' around the Christmas Tree" while the children tap dance. Mom and Dad watch from the background and sway to and fro. At the end of the dance the friends and Frosty exit stage for costume change.

Scene 5:   The three Holliday children sit down by the fireplace with Dad as Mom picks up a small manger scene. She holds it out toward them during narration as though she was telling them a story.

Curtain closes at end of "Love and peace was born that day."

ACT III

(Curtain remains closed for Act III): The seven friends and Frosty are backstage changing costumes. They will become the Living Nativity.

Scene 1:   Carolers sing "O Little Town of Bethlehem."

Scene 2:   As carolers sing "It Came upon a Midnight Clear," an angel appears on stage.

Scene 3:   As carolers sing verse one of "Silent Night," Mary and Joseph enter center stage. As carolers sing verse two of "Silent Night," two shepherds enter stage. As carolers sing verse three of "Silent Night," three kings enter stage.

ACT IV (curtain opens)

Scene 1:   Sitting in the living room is Santa and the Holliday family. The Living Nativity and carolers all join the Holliday family in the living room as a child soloist sings "Silver Bells."

THE END

8Bo CLAY ORNAMENTS - NO BAKE METHOD

Materials You Need:

- 1½ cups water
- 2 cups salt
- 1 cup cornstarch
- Saucepan
- Mixing bowl
- Wax paper

- Toothpick
- Cooling rack
- Acrylic paint
- Paint brush
- Cookie cutters
- Rolling pin

How You Make It:

1. Mix salt and cornstarch in mixing bowl.
2. Bring water to a boil in saucepan; remove from heat.
3. Slowly add salt and cornstarch mixture to water while stirring.
4. Return mixture to low heat and continue to cook until dough is hard to stir.
5. Remove from pan.
6. Place on wax paper and let cool.
7. Knead till smooth.
8. Roll out dough to ⅛-inch thickness and cut with cookie cutters or create free-form design.
9. Poke a hole in top of ornament with a toothpick.
10. Place ornaments on cooling racks and let dry (two to three days).
11. When dry, paint. Let paint dry.
12. Attach string through hole in top of ornament for hanging.

ELBOW

PINKY

ROLLING PIN

KA-CHUNK   KA-CHUNK   KA-CHUNK

WAX PAPER

More Ideas for You:

Store unused clay in airtight container or zip-lock bag with air removed.

83 E-Z EGGNOG PUNCH

Materials You Need:

- 1 gallon eggnog
- ½ gallon vanilla ice cream
- Punch bowl
- Knife
- Nutmeg

How You Make It:

1. Cut ½ gallon of vanilla ice cream into four pieces with knife.

2. Put ice cream pieces in punch bowl.

3. Pour one gallon eggnog over ice cream. Ice cream keeps this punch cold and creamy for several hours.

4. Sprinkle nutmeg over punch.

More Ideas for You:

To create a beautiful centerpiece for a party, set punch bowl filled with "E-Z Eggnog Punch" in center of a green Christmas wreath decorated with shiny red Christmas balls.

84o GIFT TAGS

Materials You Need:

- Colored construction paper
- Scissors
- Pencil
- Christmas cookie cutters
- Single-hole paper punch
- Colored yarn

How You Make It:

1. Trace a cookie cutter onto colored construction paper. Cut out.

2. Punch a hole in top of shape.

3. Attach a piece of colored yarn through hole to tie onto gift.

4. On one side of the shape write the word *TO:*

5. On the other side of the shape write the word *FROM:*

85. GINGERBREAD MAN ORNAMENT

Materials You Need:

- Approximately 4-inch tall gingerbread man cookie cutter
- Piece of corrugated cardboard or brown construction paper
- Colored yarn for trim and hanger
- Colored paper (your choice—for buttons, cheeks, and eyes)
- Single-hole paper punch
- Scissors
- Glue
- Pencil

How You Make It:

1. Trace the gingerbread man on cardboard or construction paper using cookie cutter and pencil.

2. Cut out the man.

3. Tie a piece of the colored yarn in a bow and glue to neck edge; glue pieces of yarn to arms and legs to look like frosting; make yarn mouth. Let dry.

4. Using punch, cut small circles out of colored paper to make two eyes, two cheeks, and three belly buttons.

5. Glue circles on man. Let dry.

6. Punch a single hole in top of man and thread yarn through hole and tie in a knot to form hanger.

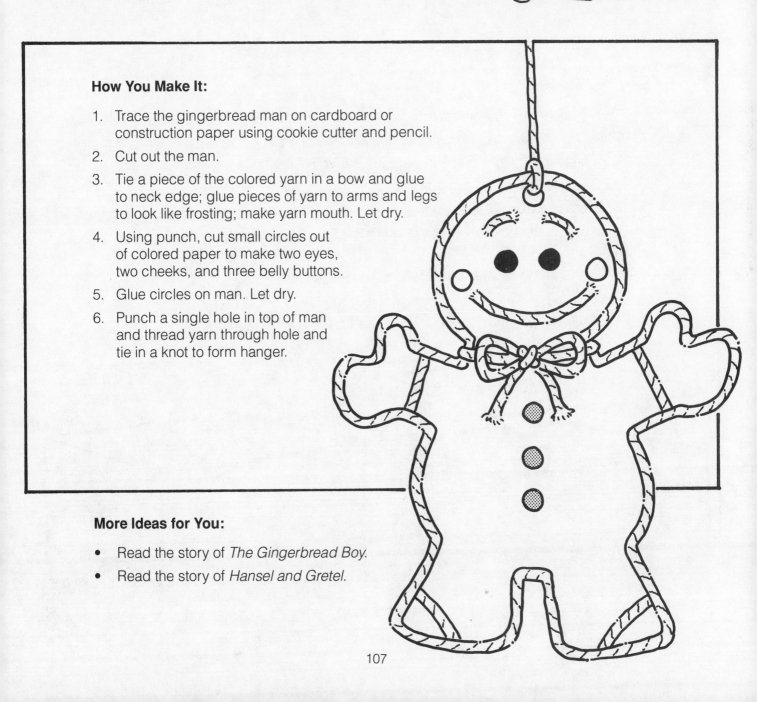

More Ideas for You:

- Read the story of *The Gingerbread Boy.*
- Read the story of *Hansel and Gretel.*

86. GLITTER STENCIL GIFT WRAP

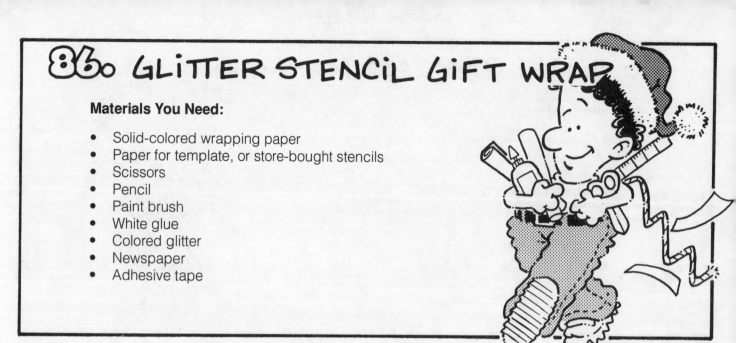

Materials You Need:

- Solid-colored wrapping paper
- Paper for template, or store-bought stencils
- Scissors
- Pencil
- Paint brush
- White glue
- Colored glitter
- Newspaper
- Adhesive tape

How You Make It:

1. Cover work area with newspaper.
2. Trace and cut design or letters for template from paper, or buy ready-made stencils.
3. Wrap present with solid-colored wrapping paper. Secure ends with adhesive tape.
4. Lay template on top of wrapped gift.
5. Brush on a thin film of white glue.
6. While glue is still tacky, shake glitter onto design and press it gently with your fingers.
7. Shake excess glitter onto newspaper so it can be recovered and re-used.
8. Let glitter stencil dry.

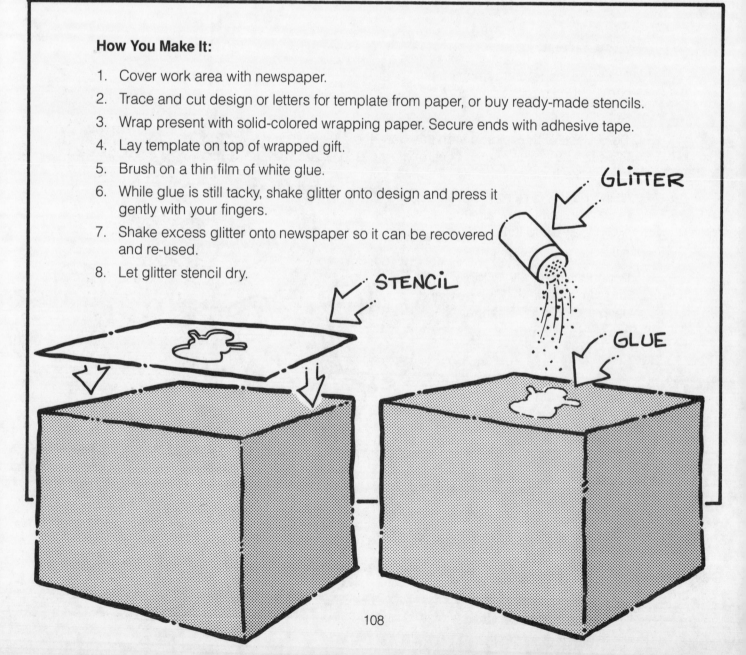

GLITTER

STENCIL

GLUE

87. JEWELRY TREE

Materials You Need:

- 9" x 11" piece of cardboard
- 9" x 11" piece of green felt
- 9" x 11" wooden picture frame
- Tacky glue
- Old costume jewelry (may be purchased at thrift stores)
- Sequins or beads
- Narrow lace
- Small piece of red ribbon

How You Make It:

1. Glue corners of green felt to cardboard.

2. Insert cardboard and felt into wooden picture frame.

3. Glue thin necklace chains to felt to resemble a triangular Christmas tree.

4. Decorate tree by gluing jewelry, sequins, or beads in place.

5. Glue narrow lace around inside edge of picture frame.

6. Make a small bow from ribbon and glue in center of top lace.

7. Let dry.

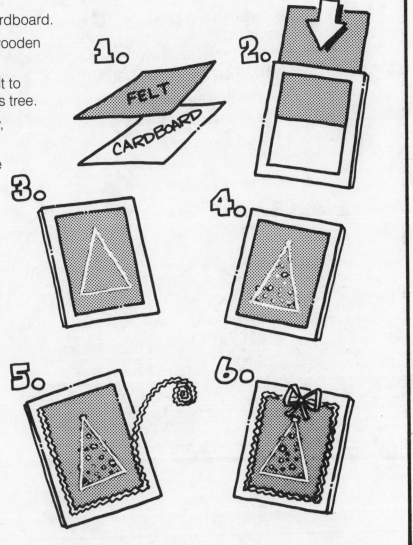

88 o MACARONI GARLAND

Materials You Need:

- Small tubular macaroni (often called "salad macaroni")
- Wagon wheel macaroni
- Needle
- Thread or crochet cotton

How You Make It:

1. Thread needle with about three yards of button thread or crochet cotton.

2. Secure end by bringing thread end out of, and then back around through tubular macaroni. Tie thread in knot.

3. Alternate tubular and wagon wheel macaroni to form garland.

4. End by following step #2.

TIE A KNOT HERE...
TWO OR EVEN
THREE TIMES
IF NEEDED.

89. MACARONI SNOWFLAKE

Materials You Need:

- Assorted macaroni (wagon wheel, shell, elbow, bow tie, etc.)
- Glue
- Scissors
- Colored construction paper
- Acrylic paint (optional)
- Wax paper
- Yarn or ribbon
- Paint brush
- Glitter (optional)

How You Make It:

1. Cover work area with large piece of wax paper.

2. Place a small amount of glue on one corner of wax paper.

3. Dip pieces of macaroni in the glue and stick them together in the shape of a snowflake.

4. Cut out a circle of construction paper to cover the snowflake and glue the snowflake to it. Let dry.

5. Paint edges of macaroni with acrylic paint, if desired. While paint is still wet, sprinkle with glitter. Let dry.

6. Make a hole in top of construction paper and thread yarn or ribbon through.

7. The snowflake may be worn as a necklace or used as a Christmas tree decoration.

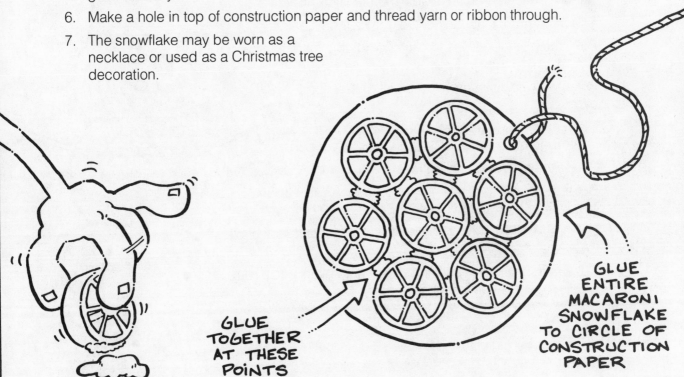

GLUE

GLUE TOGETHER AT THESE POINTS

GLUE ENTIRE MACARONI SNOWFLAKE TO CIRCLE OF CONSTRUCTION PAPER

⚙ MARSHMALLOW SNOWMAN

Materials You Need:

- 3 large marshmallows per snowman
- 5 whole cloves per snowman
- Toothpicks
- Red candy gumdrops
- Ribbon
- Black construction paper
- Sugar cookies
- Canned white frosting

How You Make It:

1. Put a dab of frosting on sugar cookie.

2. Lay a marshmallow on its side on the frosting.

3. Insert a toothpick through center of marshmallow.

4. Attach a second marshmallow onto toothpick.

5. Insert a toothpick through second marshmallow.

6. Attach a third marshmallow on second toothpick.

7. Attach two toothpicks in middle marshmallow for arms.

8. Attach gumdrops at ends of toothpicks for mittens.

9. Poke three whole cloves in center of middle marshmallow for buttons.

10. Poke two whole cloves in top marshmallow for eyes.

11. Cut a gumdrop in quarters and attach a quarter gumdrop on a toothpick for nose.

12. Tie a ribbon around neck for scarf.

13. Cut a circle from black construction paper a little larger in circumference than top marshmallow.

14. Using a small amount of frosting as glue, attach black circle to top marshmallow.

15. Cut a marshmallow in half and glue it onto black circle with a small amount of frosting for hat.

𝅘𝅥𝅮 MINIATURE CHRISTMAS TREE GARLAND

Materials You Need:

- Gummed stars
- Heavy thread or thin yarn
- Scissors

How You Make It:

1. Attach two gummed stars back-to-back on a piece of thread. (Thread is positioned between backs of stars.)

2. Continue to attach stars about every inch on thread.

3. Garland may be made as long as you like.

4. Cut thread when desired length is reached.

5. Garland is a great decoration for a miniature Christmas tree.

THREAD

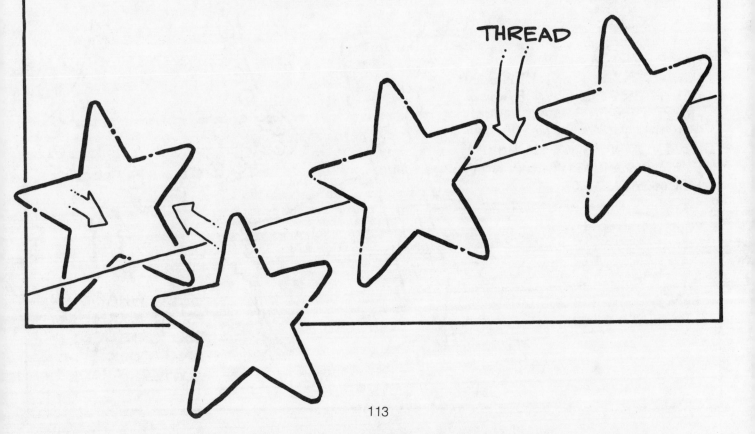

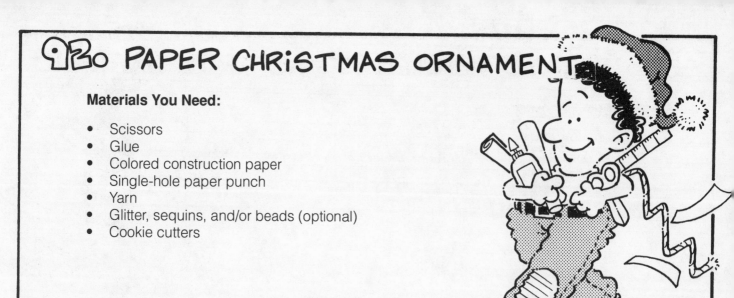

120 PAPER CHRISTMAS ORNAMENT

Materials You Need:

- Scissors
- Glue
- Colored construction paper
- Single-hole paper punch
- Yarn
- Glitter, sequins, and/or beads (optional)
- Cookie cutters

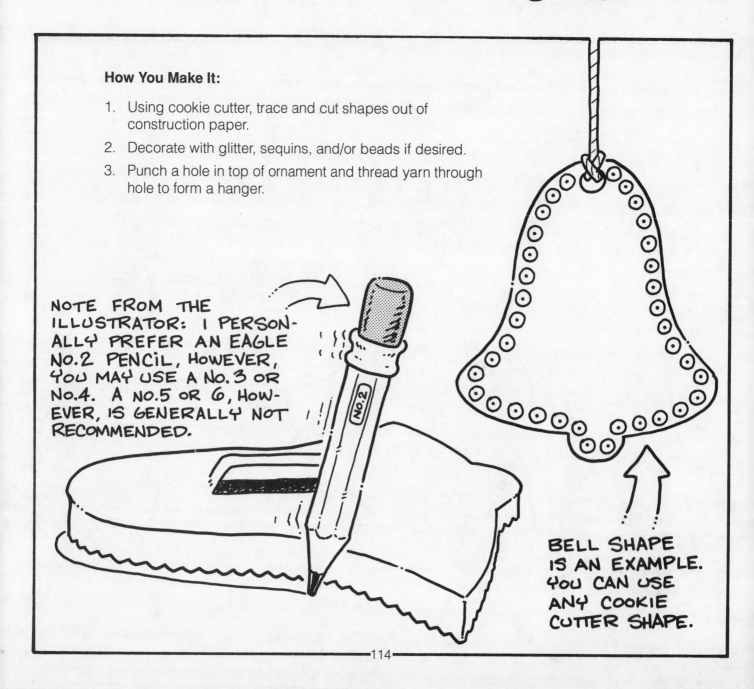

How You Make It:

1. Using cookie cutter, trace and cut shapes out of construction paper.

2. Decorate with glitter, sequins, and/or beads if desired.

3. Punch a hole in top of ornament and thread yarn through hole to form a hanger.

NOTE FROM THE ILLUSTRATOR: I PERSONALLY PREFER AN EAGLE NO.2 PENCIL, HOWEVER, YOU MAY USE A NO.3 OR NO.4. A NO.5 OR 6, HOWEVER, IS GENERALLY NOT RECOMMENDED.

NO.2

BELL SHAPE IS AN EXAMPLE. YOU CAN USE ANY COOKIE CUTTER SHAPE.

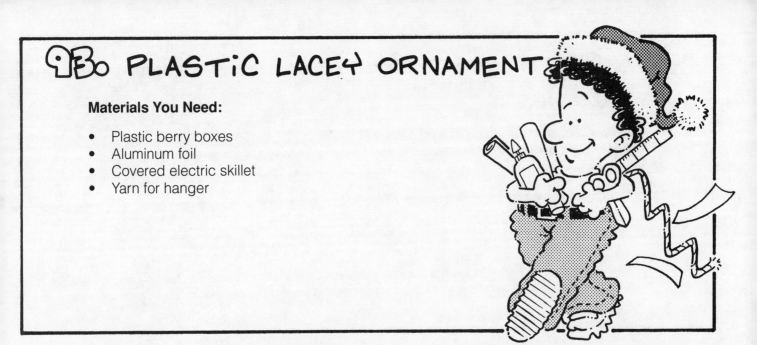

130 PLASTIC LACEY ORNAMENT

Materials You Need:

- Plastic berry boxes
- Aluminum foil
- Covered electric skillet
- Yarn for hanger

How You Make It:

1. Place a sheet of foil in bottom of electric skillet.

2. Lay plastic berry box upside down on foil.

3. Put cover on skillet.

4. Turn temperature control to 250 degrees.

5. Heat until plastic box begins to melt. Check occasionally under *adult supervision*.

6. Remove from heat when plastic box reaches desired lacey form.

7. To hang, thread yarn through an opening in "Plastic Lacey Ornament."

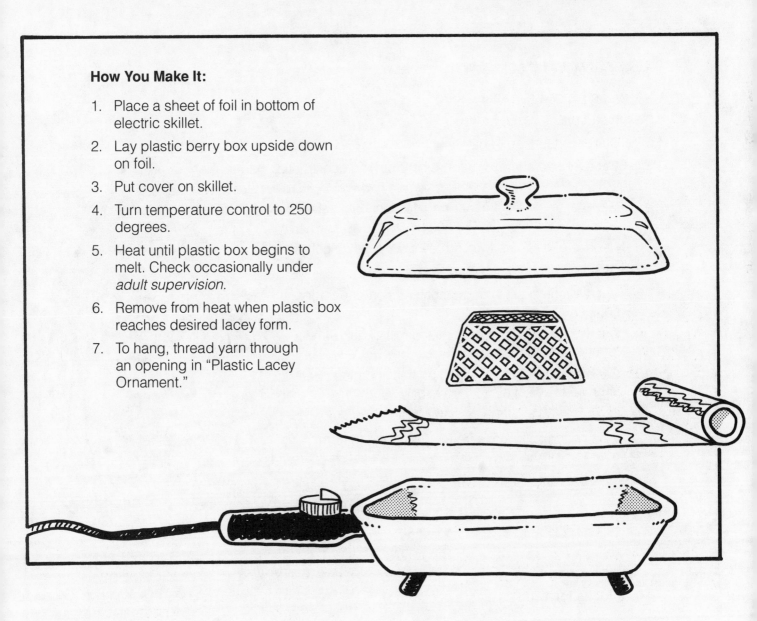

94o SANTA GiFT BAG

Materials You Need:

- Large brown paper bag (with no advertisements)
- Red and pink construction paper
- Black yarn
- Red yarn
- White cotton balls
- Stapler or adhesive tape
- Glue
- Scissors

How You Make It:

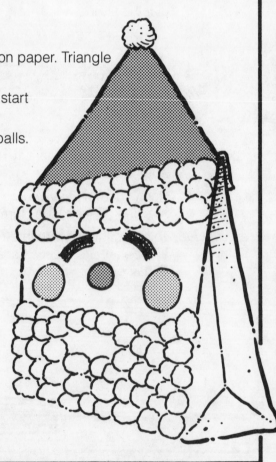

1. Open large brown paper bag.
2. Insert gift.
3. Staple or tape top of bag shut.
4. Cut a large triangle for Santa's hat from red construction paper. Triangle bottom should be the same width as the paper bag.
5. Glue hat to top $\frac{1}{4}$ of paper bag. Bottom of hat should start about three inches from top of the bag.
6. At base of hat, glue two or three rows of white cotton balls.
7. Glue one cotton ball on point of hat.
8. Cut a 1-inch circle from red construction paper for a nose and glue in place.
9. Cut two 2-inch circles from pink construction paper for cheeks and glue in place.
10. Cut black yarn into six 4-inch pieces and glue three each in a semi-circle to form happy eyes.
11. Cut red yarn and form into smile. Glue in place.
12. Glue cotton balls along bottom $\frac{1}{3}$ of bag to form beard.
13. Let dry.

More Ideas for You:

A smaller Santa gift bag may also be made by using a brown sandwich bag.

95. SHINY SPIRALS

Materials You Need:

- Paper
- Pencil
- Scissors
- Glue
- Glitter
- Newspaper
- Christmas tree ornament hook

How You Make It:

1. Cover work area with newspaper.
2. Draw a spiral on a piece of paper.
3. Cut along the spiral line.
4. When spiral is cut, lay it down to flat position.
5. Drizzle glue on spiral.
6. Sprinkle glitter on glue.
7. Attach a Christmas tree hook to one end of the spiral.
8. Hang to dry.
9. Be sure to save and re-use excess glitter.

AFTER GLUED AND GLITTERED, PUT A HOOK IN CENTER AND HANG.

96. SILVER BELLS

Materials You Need:

- 3 paper cups
- Aluminum foil
- Ribbon (about 4 feet long by $\frac{1}{2}$ to 1 inch wide)
- Scissors
- 3 jingle bells
- Pencil
- Stapler with staples

How You Make It:

1. Turn paper cup upside down.
2. Punch a hole in the bottom of the cup with a pencil.
3. Cut a piece of ribbon about 12 inches long.
4. Push one end of ribbon down through the hole of the cup.
5. Turn cup over and pull ribbon through the cup.
6. Tie a jingle bell to the end of the ribbon.
7. Make a large knot about two inches from the jingle bell. Make sure knot is large enough to not go through the hole in the cup.
8. Turn the cup upside down again and pull the ribbon up toward you. The knot will keep the ribbon from slipping through the hole.
9. Cut a piece of aluminum foil large enough to cover the paper cup.
10. Wrap the foil tightly around the top and sides of the cup.
11. Fold extra foil under the rim and press it firmly to the inside of the cup.
12. Repeat steps 1 through 11 with remaining two cups.
13. When three bells are completed, vary lengths and staple three ribbon ends together.
14. Cut another piece of ribbon and tie into a bow.
15. Staple bow to bell ribbon ends.

PULL UP

97o SOAPY ORNAMENT

Materials You Need:

- Posterboard, cardboard, or construction paper
- Scissors
- Paint brush
- Liquid starch
- Soap flakes
- Glitter
- Yarn or ribbon for hangers
- Single-hole paper punch

How You Make It:

1. Cut assorted shapes (snowman, tree, star, snowflake) from poster-board, or construction paper.

2. Punch a hole in top of the shape and attach yarn or ribbon for hanger.

3. Paint shape with liquid starch.

4. Dip painted shape in soap flakes.

5. Sprinkle with glitter.

6. Hang to dry.

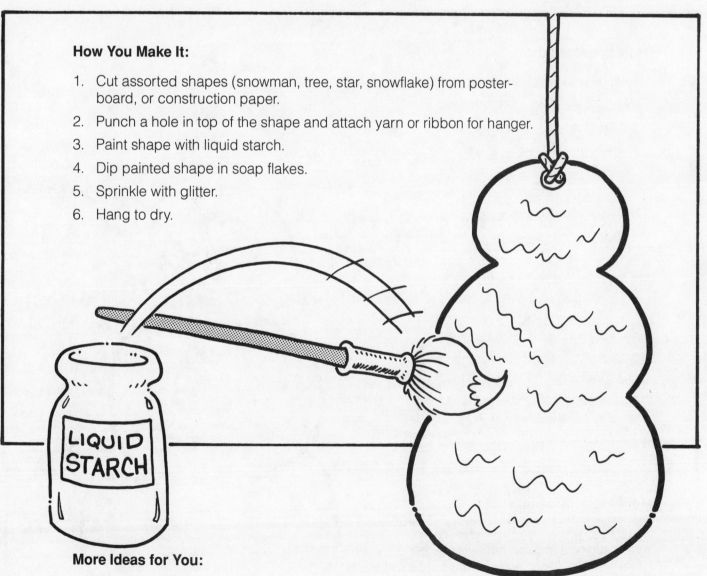

More Ideas for You:

If you have access to an overhead projector, shapes may be enlarged to be used as large indoor and outdoor decorations.

98. SOAPY SNOWMAN SCULPTURE

Materials You Need:

- 2 cups soap flakes
- ¼ cup water
- Large bowl
- Refrigerator
- Wax paper
- Acrylic paint
- Paint brush

How You Make It:

1. Cover work area with wax paper.
2. Put soap flakes in large bowl.
3. Add water.
4. Mix soap flakes and water with your hands until mixture is damp and squishy.
5. Mixture is ready to sculpt when it sticks together.
6. Pour mixture on wax paper.
7. Form a snowman by making three balls.
8. Place balls one on top of each other, pressing gently so they stick together.
9. Put snowman in the refrigerator for several hours until firm. Handle the sculpture very carefully until it is completely dry and firm.
10. When sculpture is dry and firm, paint eyes, nose, mouth and buttons. Let dry.
11. Finished sculpture may be used as a decoration or as a soapy friend at bathtime.

CAN YOU PAINT THIS FACE?

More Ideas for You:

Soapy sculpture may be made into any shape. After sculpture is firm, dab a little water on it and gently sprinkle with dry soap flakes. Soap flakes will stick to the wet surface and create a fluffy, furry effect especially cute for animal sculptures.

99. Stocking Sewing Cards

Materials You Need:

- 9" x 12" piece of posterboard or cardboard
- Pencil
- Crayons
- Single-hole paper punch
- Colored yarn
- Scissors
- Tape

How You Make It:

1. Draw a large stocking shape onto posterboard or cardboard.

2. Color stocking.

3. With single-hole paper punch, punch holes evenly spaced around outside edge of shape.

4. Cut a piece of yarn about three feet long.

5. Wrap a small piece of tape on each end of yarn to make sewing through holes easier.

6. Starting at top of stocking, begin running yarn through holes.

7. When finished, use excess yarn to form a hanger for your stocking. Stocking may be hung on the Christmas tree, wall, or window.

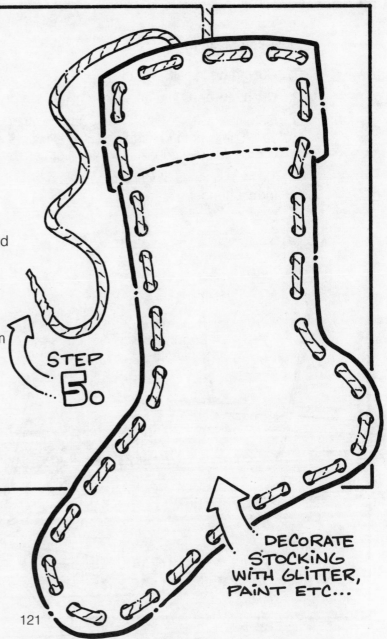

STEP 5.

DECORATE STOCKING WITH GLITTER, PAINT ETC...

More Ideas for You:

Christmas trees, snowmen, stars, and teddy bears are a few more shapes you could make.

100. STRAW BURST DECORATION

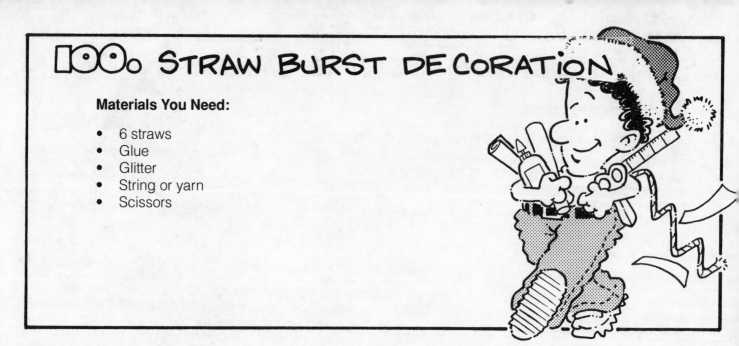

Materials You Need:

- 6 straws
- Glue
- Glitter
- String or yarn
- Scissors

How You Make It:

1. Cut straws in half.

2. Dip straw ends in glue, then in glitter. Let dry.

3. Gather straws together evenly and tie string or yarn tightly around middle, bending straws as you tie. Make a tight knot in string or yarn.

4. Tie excess ends of string or yarn in a loop to form a hanger.

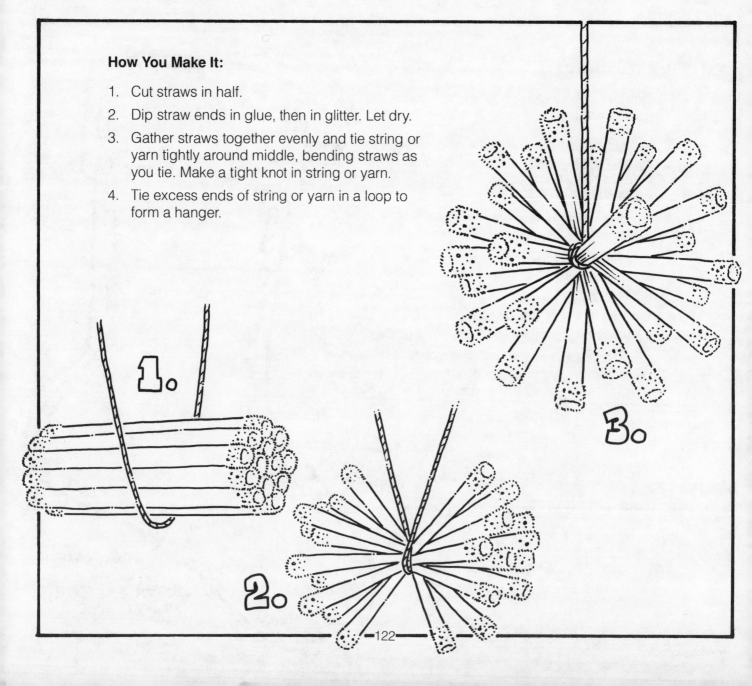

o SWEET 'N SPICY POMANDER

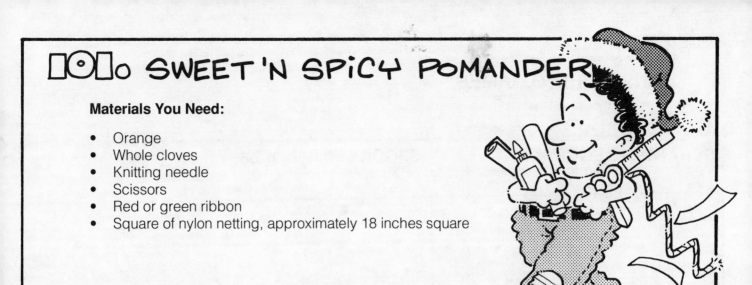

Materials You Need:

- Orange
- Whole cloves
- Knitting needle
- Scissors
- Red or green ribbon
- Square of nylon netting, approximately 18 inches square

How You Make It:

1. Poke evenly-spaced holes all over an orange with a knitting needle, being careful to make them just deep enough to break the skin.

2. Stick the clove stems into the holes.

3. Lay the orange in the center of the square of nylon netting.

4. Bring ends of netting up firmly around the orange.

5. Tie netting firmly at top of orange with ribbon.

6. Hang pomander in a closet or room for a sweet and spicy fragrance.

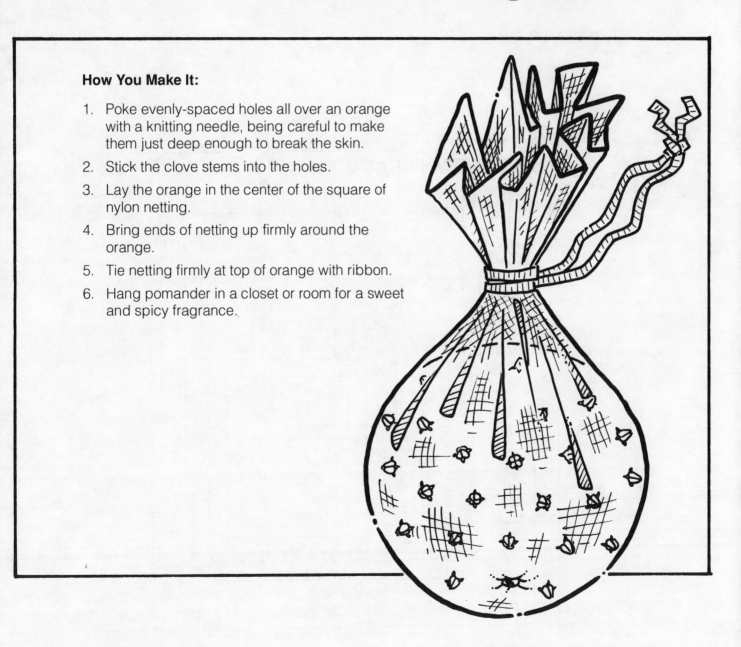

ANSWERS TO GAMES

SCRAMBLED EGGS, p. 11

```
B A S K E T
E G G S
C H O C O L A T E
G R A S S
C H I C K
L I L Y
J E L L Y    B E A N S
E G G    H U N T
B O N N E T
B U N N Y
```

SPOOKY FILL-IN, p. 56

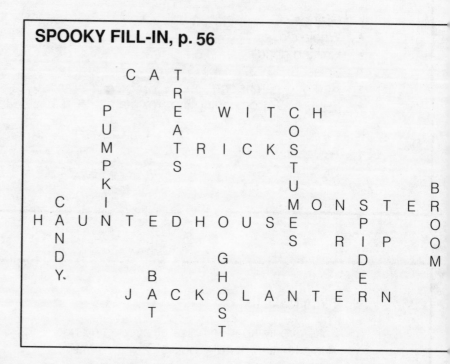

```
              C A T       T
                          R E A T S        W I T C H       H
              P                            T               O
              U                            R I C K S        C S
              M                            E                 T
              P                            A                 U
              K                            T                 M
              I         C                  S                 E
H A U N T E D H O U S E                        M O N S T E R     B
              N       A                        S           P     R
              Y.                                           I     O
                                                           D     O
                          B A T       G H O S T            E     M
                      J A C K O L A N T E R N
                              T       S
                                      T
```

HOLIDAY SEARCH, p. 70

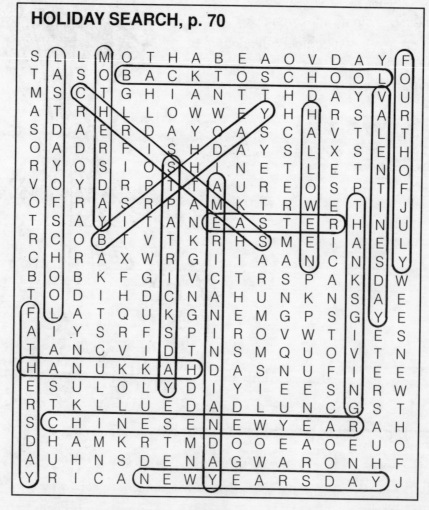

```
S L L M O T H A B E A O V D A Y F
T M A S O R V O T R C B T F A T H E R S D A Y
S S C R A D O Y R A O R B D A Y L I A N C V I
O T H E R S D A Y F I S H I N E P A R T V W G
R B A C K T O S C H O O L
V A L E N T I N E S D A Y
F O U R T H O F J U L Y
B A C K T O S C H O O L
C H I N E S E N E W Y E A R
N E W Y E A R S D A Y
H A N U K K A H
E A S T E R
H A L L O W E E N
T H A N K S G I V I N G
```

PRESIDENTIAL TOP SECRET, p. 73

```
        W A S H I N G T O N
          M A D I S O N
    K E N N E D Y N
          R E A G A N N
    L I N C O L N
          C A R T E R
T R U M A N
```

Top Secret Word: AMERICA

SECRET WORD, p. 74

```
        F A V O R I T E
        H E A R T
          L O V E
        R E D
        C A N D Y
S W E E T H E A R T
          K I S S
    P R E S E N T
    F L O W E R S
```

Secret Word: VALENTINE

CHRISTMAS CROSSWORD PUZZLE, p. 93

```
                              S                    S
                      C A N D Y      C A N         N
                      A                D            O
                      N                L            W
                      T        O       E
              W       A   C A R O L E R S
              R           N            U
              E   L F     A            D
              A           M            O
      C H R I S T M A S   S   R        L
      H       D           C   T        F
      R   E I N         C R O O G E
    D E C O R A T I O N S   O   R
      I   E   D         S   O   I
      L   E   E             G   E
      E   R   E                 S N O W M A N
              F I R E
          F R O S T         E
          G O S P E L   S L E I G H
          S T O C K I N G
          Y   A
              N
              D
              Y
```

INDEX

HOLIDAY INDEX

SICK DAYS: